Unapologetically Healing

A GUIDED JOURNAL FOR
REFLECTION AND
GENERATIONAL TRANSFORMATION

Dr. Sheila Sweeney, LICSW

Unapologetically Healing © copyright 2024 by Sheila Sweeney. All rights reserved. No part of this book may be reproduced in any form whatsoever, by photography or xerography or by any other means, by broadcast or transmission, by translation into any kind of language, nor by recording electronically or otherwise, without permission in writing from the author, except by a reviewer, who may quote brief passages in critical articles or reviews.

ISBN 13: 978-1-63489-712-9

Library of Congress Catalog Number has been applied for.
Printed in the United States of America
First Printing: 2024
28   27   26   25   24   5   4   3   2   1

Illustrations by Janay Frazier
Interior design by Janay Frazier and Vivian Steckline
Author photo by Quay Jirè Photography

Wise Ink
PO Box 580195

Minneapolis, MN 55458-0195

Wise Ink is a creative publishing agency for game-changers. Wise Ink authors uplift, inspire, and inform, and their titles support building a better and more equitable world. For more information, visit wiseink.com

To order, visit www.DrSheilaSweeney.com or call 1-800-901-3480. Reseller discounts available.

To all those who have embarked on the journey of healing, this journal is dedicated to you—

May these pages provide a safe and comforting space to explore and express your deepest thoughts and emotions. May this journal be a tool for self-discovery, growth, and transformation. May it remind you that you are not alone on this path and that there is always hope for healing.

Thank you to my family, friends, community, clients, and everyone who has influenced my thought processing along the way. I have wanted a journal since adolescence, but no journal felt perfect. They say if it does not exist, to create it. This workbook-style journal is transformative, and every reflective question included in it came from deep and genuine conversations I've had with people throughout my life.

IMPORTANT DISCLAIMER

Before engaging with this healing journal, it is crucial to prioritize your well-being and mental health. If answering these questions makes you feel distressed, unsafe, or uncertain, we strongly urge you to reach out to a mental health professional in your area. Remember, you are not alone, and there are resources available to support you.

One valuable resource is the 988 Suicide & Crisis Lifeline (formerly known as The National Suicide Prevention Lifeline), which can be reached at 988 or 1-800-273-TALK or by visiting their website at 988lifeline.org. If you are experiencing an emergency, please dial 911 in the United States or contact your local emergency services outside the United States.

It is essential to inform someone that you are engaging in this journaling process. If you are feeling suicidal or overwhelmed, please reach out to your local crisis team, hospital, or mental health provider. Your own medical provider can offer assistance and guidance. If you have a history of mental health disorders and find yourself triggered during this self-work journaling experience, we encourage you to seek support from your nearest healthcare professional.

Remember, it is perfectly acceptable to pause and return to this journal when you feel ready. This journal is intended for those who are mentally and emotionally prepared to engage in or continue their self-work, ideally in conjunction with a mental health professional. We wish you well on this journey, and it is crucial to recognize that there is no set timeline to complete this work—it is on your own time.

Please be aware that the questions in this journal were crafted with love and care, intended to foster growth rather than evoke fear. Each of us has grown up with different influences and expectations, and as you respond to these questions, we encourage you to use your own gentle voice. When you encounter overwhelming emotions, remember to take breaks and practice self-care.

Your well-being is of utmost importance.

MY UNAPOLOGETIC SELF-DECLARATION

Make a declaration that states, "Healing begins with me." With you starts the journey to a healed self, as well as healing for those who came before you and those who will come after you. Like a light shining brightly on others as one begins the healing process, the light will undoubtedly hit others as your healing shines through from the inside out. You are not your trauma. You are not what happened to you, yet you are responsible for your healing journey and the experiences that can ultimately change the trajectory of your life.

Remember, healing is a journey—and it's not easy. However, it's worth it every step of the way, as you will see once you are on the other side. Make a declaration that you will begin turning your trauma story into a healing experience that keeps going. Suffering is a part of the process, but it won't be the kind of suffering that torments you. It will be the kind of suffering that tells you this is hard, and eventually, it will be okay, and it doesn't have to be easy to feel okay.

I, _____, declare that healing begins with me. I am responsible for my healing, and I do not need to rely on anybody else to begin the process of moving from traumatic experiences into healing experiences that matter to me.

I will give myself permission to heal and move forward in whatever way I see fit.

I will keep what works for me, and I will discard what doesn't, as well as what is seemingly holding me back in my progression on this healing journey.

I understand I may be the pioneer in this work, and that other people may be involved in what I am healing from or healing toward. When I pause and need a moment to breathe through it, take it in, digest it, and push over walls and boundaries that stand in my way, I will offer myself grace.

I also recognize that this is a process, and that it will take time. I grant myself the time and space that I need through incremental steps to move forward in my healing journey.

I thank myself in advance for the process and progress from the result of this self-work. I deserve to be healed. I deserve to be whole. I deserve to be a holistic, unapologetic me. I am not what happened to me; and I will, to the best of my ability, reject things that I know could be harmful to my loved ones.

If I stumble and make mistakes along the way, I will pause, forgive myself, give myself grace, and keep moving forward. On this journey, though sometimes I might take steps backward, I know that this is normal and that is also okay. All of this will be my story to tell, both along the way and when all is said and done.

Signature: _____ Date: _____

Take three deep breaths to reset as needed!

Dear reader,

I am proud of you for starting or continuing your healing journey and experiences.

I wish you well, I pray good things for you, and I know your healing experience will speak volumes to your future self.

See you on the other side,

Sheila
xoxoxo

Contents

Introduction and Warm-Up — 4

Your Journey Begins Here — 17

A Better Vibe, a Better Life — 73

Gathering to Grow — 129

Healing the Narrative — 181

Level Up and Thrive — 239

Recall and Recap — 299

Crowning Glory — 357

Your Journey Continues — 364

Author Resources — 386

Acknowledgments — 390

Pause Moment #1

**Pause often. Reset often—
pivot as needed.**

**Unpack your stuff,
and *name your emotions*, as
you move on.**

Take three deep breaths to reset as needed!

Notice your breath. As you notice, breathe in and out without doing anything different; for now, you are simply noticing your breath . . . notice the rise and fall of your chest, your belly, and whether you typically breathe through your nose or your mouth . . . no judgment, breathe.

Hold in Mind

Let's begin the healing process, no matter what stage you are at. Because guess what? I'm doing it too, right along with you. Although I have written these questions with thoughtfulness and care, I, too, go back through them so I can make sure I am checking with my inner being and answering for what today's responses would be. Because let me tell you something: I have learned time and time again that I am not the same person I was before I began my own healing journey.

Just Write . . . and Don't Judge

Don't second-guess yourself or judge your responses as you work in this journal. Let the words come out, and guard them if you need to. But let it come out, then elaborate. This is for YOU. As long as you can read your writing, it's good enough—because you are good enough.

Also, don't worry about returning to these pages. Let them call you in to do the work when your mind, body, and spirit are drawn to do so. And don't hesitate to push yourself to write on days when you may be operating from an empty cup. Writing in this journal is meant to be a judgment-free zone. Give yourself permission to come back as often as you like, as time goes on, or as conversations with yourself and other people tell you to grab this journal.

Finally, let's use this journal to create wonderful memories while discarding those that no longer serve you. When something doesn't make sense or you want to do something different while writing, pivot.

Recognize the Patterns When You Write (or Afterward)

When you return to this journal, take note of the dates. Is there a pattern when you explore similar topics? Do you write for a longer period of time when this happens? Or for a shorter period of time?

Also, how do you feel when you're journaling in these moments? Do you, for instance, write unapologetically? Fearlessly? With more freedom? Or do you write from an anxious place?

THE SOUNDTRACK
(OR PLAYLIST) OF YOUR JOURNAL

Why not listen to your favorite tunes while you journal and create a soundtrack for your journal? It can be whatever you want. Use the spaces below to write down a few of your favorite artists and songs to get you started on your journaling journey.

You can list songs along the way and, eventually, your full soundtrack or playlist. Each question has a tone and mood-setting page where you have space to write down what you are listening to while answering each specific question. Additionally, see page 366 at the end of this journal, where you will find another place to list your full soundtrack.

Song	Artist

Set the Mood and Tone for Your Journaling First

Imagine your favorite candle or scent, your favorite beverage, your favorite warm or sexy clothing, and a great writing utensil. What do you love writing with? For example, do you prefer a nice set of pens, a tablet, or a mobile device? Or do you prefer your computer? Do you love to listen to your favorite fly tunes playing in the background when you pull this journal out, or does silence set the mood just right?

When you set the tone for your journaling, here are a few physical items you may pay attention to—and even list in each journal entry.

- What does the weather look like outside? What is the temperature or weather like?
- Where are you right now as you write?
- What song is playing? Or, are you singing anything?
- What are you doing as you write?
- What kind of mood are you in?
- Are you drinking anything?
- Do a quick body scan. Where are you in your body? Your mind? Your spirit?
- What do you want to remember about your writing experience today?
- Do you give yourself full permission to write unapologetically?
- Are you going to keep writing today after you finish the current page? If yes, put today's date on the following page and keep writing.

Remember to set your mental tone, too. Whose voice do you hear when you write? Who do you think will know what you wrote about? Pay attention to your thoughts so you can make sure that, as you start this process, these thoughts are yours. These words that you write in this journal are yours. Your feelings and fears are yours. Give yourself permission to write from your own story and reassign (or assign) the voices of others right back to them. Their thoughts are not your thoughts. Again, whose voice is it anyway? Do you like the voice that's speaking through your memories right now? If so, explain why. If not, why not? Keep what works and discard the rest. And if you're unsure, know that it's okay to work through this portion of your thoughts and memories as your psyche allows.

Drop the pen and read what you wrote when you're finished journaling. What do you think? You made part of the soundtrack to your journal by recording these details of your writing adventure, which include tone and mood, along with the musical tunes, silence, or sounds that are in the space.

On the following page is an example of how I set the mood and tone for a journaling session. This is also an example or reference to assist you in envisioning your tone and mood as you journal.

AN EXAMPLE OF SETTING THE MOOD AND TONE BEFORE JOURNALING

Today: 12/28/2022

I'm drinking Riesling on a staycation (home).

I'm listening to Musiq Soulchild and Anthony Hamilton on Pandora, no TV.

My candle is called LOVE. Smells good!

My writing utensils are a laptop, a pen, and paper.

The vibe is chill. I'm excited and tearful, plus hopeful.

The temp outside is brrrrrr in Minnesota—snowy and thirty degrees. The heat is turned up because I am loving this task of writing this journal for you!

I'm sitting on the countertop and feeling sexy in my fitted workout clothes because I'm pretending that after writing, I will go and work out. ;)

I do this work with my higher power in mind, knowing that's where my true healing comes from, and this is supplemental work to assist in my earthly walk of self-healing and worth! I do not believe we alone have the power to heal ourselves. This is the work we are doing to supplement the work that has been put inside of us already.

Healing begins with me.
Healing continues with me.
I am not my trauma.
I am not the drama that surrounds me.

Introduction and Warm-Up

SAMPLE

Set the Mood and Tone for Today's Journaling

Date and Time: *Mon 8/9/23 5pm*
(Write the date and time here)

Location: *@home chillin*
(Write where you are physically located today)

Today my sound choice is: *Both silence and music; I like DC's radio station WPGC.*
(Write down your sound choice for your journaling experience today; examples: silence, music, something else)

Smells, if any: *Diffuser*   Drinking or eating anything: *Water and green tea*

I am looking at and noticing *How beautiful it is outside in Aug + sunshine* surrounding me.

Tasks I accomplished today: *I worked, rested, meditated, and worked out today (yay).*

How accomplished I feel today: 1   2   3   (**4**)   5
(Circle the number that you resonate with. 1 = a mess 2 = meh 3 = I'm okay 4 = I'm good 5 = I'm a masterpiece)

I am taking a break from *My reflective groups today*. I give myself permission to get back up and start *Prepping the rest of the week* again on/at *tomorrow*.
(Write the name of the task or activity, then write the expected date for returning to this task or activity)

Check in to check out: What other emotions or things am I experiencing today?
I am realizing how much I need to get done for the month, yet I have time to add rest moments!

My latest self-takeaway: *I realize I must believe it and move my positive thoughts forward . . .*

Reflection: What do I want to remember from the last question I focused on?

I focused on the question about asking for help. It is so hard for me to ask for help. It stems from my childhood and being told constantly to be quiet by adults. I figured things out on my own a lot, and so now, to not be dismissed by others, I avoid asking for the support I need, big or little things. I'm working on asking what I need and when, but it is hard. I deserve support! xoxoxoxo to me.

Let's Get Started

Imagine this journal is for you. You who want to do some informal work outside of a therapist or mental health professional. Healing begins with you, and you are connected to others. As you hold others in your mind while you journal through your healing experience, do not allow the other's voice to define how you respond to each question. Remember, you grew up with different voices and tasks for what to do and what not to do. Continue to use your own gentle voice to respond to the questions and reject the harsh and intolerable voices. Those voices are not yours. Please return them to whoever they belong to. Focus on the supportive individuals you will continually keep in mind while you do this important work. These individuals are the people who make up your healing village.

Please choose any question from the following pages and focus on answering one journal entry at a time. Before each journal entry—or set of entries—you will find a Set the Mood and Tone worksheet to help you prepare. Remember to take your time. Be kind and gentle with yourself as you think over certain questions. Answer the questions when you're ready.

Introduction and Warm-Up

PRE-QUESTIONS:

THE WARM-UP

Before the Journaling Journey

What brings you here? Why now?

_____
_____
_____
_____
_____
_____
_____
_____

How are you doing? Now, how are you really doing?

_____
_____
_____
_____
_____
_____
_____
_____

How do you care for yourself?

Moment-to-moment self-care matters! This can look like sips of water; short, gentle movements; standing up; giving yourself grace and space; pausing before responding; forgiveness for making mistakes; forgiveness for falling for it again; or forgiveness and healing for not knowing (or for never knowing because you are still growing).

_____
_____
_____
_____
_____
_____
_____
_____
_____
_____
_____
_____
_____
_____

Pause Moment #2

Health and healing are birthrights.

Claim yours today.

**Breathe in what's good.
Breathe out what you no longer need.
Let it go!**

Next, inhale until your lungs fill, then fully release your breath with intention.
Repeat that two more times, each time deepening your inhale and exhale if you can.

Your Journey Begins Here

Set the Mood and Tone for Today's Journaling

Date and Time: _____   Location: _____.

Today my sound choice is: _____.

Smells, if any: _____ Drinking or eating anything: _____.

I am looking at and noticing _____ surrounding me.

Tasks I accomplished today: _____.

How accomplished I feel today: 1   2   3   4   5

I am taking a break from _____. I give myself permission to get back up and start _____ again on/at _____.

Check in to check out: What other emotions or things am I experiencing today?
_____.

My latest self-takeaway: _____.

Reflection: What do I want to remember from the last question I focused on?

_____

_____

_____

_____

_____

_____

_____

Your Journey Begins Here

1. Do you believe in a higher power?

   a. If so, what or who is it? Is this the same higher power you believed in as a child? Or have you pivoted to a different one?

   b. Are you satisfied with your spiritual journey? Or are there things you still need to work on?

   c. How do you know you are connected to the right source? What tells you either way? How do you reconnect with your source when you feel disconnected or discontent with where you are?

Set the Mood and Tone for Today's Journaling

Date and Time: _____ Location: _____.

Today my sound choice is: _____

Smells, if any: _____ Drinking or eating anything: _____.

I am looking at and noticing _____ surrounding me.

Tasks I accomplished today: _____.

How accomplished I feel today: 1   2   3   4   5

I am taking a break from _____. I give myself permission to get back up and start _____ again on/at _____.

Check in to check out: What other emotions or things am I experiencing today?
_____.

My latest self-takeaway: _____.

Reflection: What do I want to remember from the last question I focused on?

_____
_____
_____
_____
_____
_____
_____

2. Do you have your own faith walk or path? Or do you still follow what you were brought up to believe? Is it still working for you? How do you know?

___

Set the Mood and Tone for Today's Journaling

Date and Time: _____ Location: _____.

Today my sound choice is: _____

Smells, if any: _____ Drinking or eating anything: _____.

I am looking at and noticing _____ surrounding me.

Tasks I accomplished today: _____.

How accomplished I feel today: 1   2   3   4   5

I am taking a break from _____. I give myself permission to get back up and start _____ again on/at _____.

Check in to check out: What other emotions or things am I experiencing today?
_____.

My latest self-takeaway: _____.

Reflection: What do I want to remember from the last question I focused on?

_____
_____
_____
_____
_____
_____
_____
_____

3. Do you ever think you are supposed to be further along in your journey? Or be more than what you are now? What tells you this?

_____
_____
_____
_____
_____
_____
_____
_____
_____
_____
_____
_____
_____
_____
_____
_____
_____

Set the Mood and Tone for Today's Journaling

Date and Time: _____   Location: _____.

Today my sound choice is: _____

Smells, if any: _____ Drinking or eating anything: _____.

I am looking at and noticing _____ surrounding me.

Tasks I accomplished today: _____.

How accomplished I feel today: 1   2   3   4   5

I am taking a break from _____. I give myself permission to get

back up and start _____ again on/at _____.

Check in to check out: What other emotions or things am I experiencing today?
_____.

My latest self-takeaway: _____.

Reflection: What do I want to remember from the last question I focused on?

_____

_____

_____

_____

_____

_____

_____

Your Journey Begins Here

4. What haunts you? Or taunts you? What hurts you?

Set the Mood and Tone for Today's Journaling

Date and Time: _____ Location: _____.

Today my sound choice is: _____

Smells, if any: _____ Drinking or eating anything: _____.

I am looking at and noticing _____ surrounding me.

Tasks I accomplished today: _____.

How accomplished I feel today: 1   2   3   4   5

I am taking a break from _____. I give myself permission to get

back up and start _____ again on/at _____.

Check in to check out: What other emotions or things am I experiencing today?
_____.

My latest self-takeaway: _____.

Reflection: What do I want to remember from the last question I focused on?

_____

_____

_____

_____

_____

_____

_____

Your Journey Begins Here

5. Do you give yourself praise? Or permission to do something (or stop doing something)? Do you give yourself small or big celebrations? Is this countercultural to your upbringing?

_____
_____
_____
_____
_____
_____
_____
_____
_____
_____
_____
_____
_____
_____
_____
_____
_____
_____
_____
_____

Set the Mood and Tone for Today's Journaling

Date and Time: _____ Location: _____.

Today my sound choice is: _____

Smells, if any: _____ Drinking or eating anything: _____.

I am looking at and noticing _____ surrounding me.

Tasks I accomplished today: _____.

How accomplished I feel today: 1   2   3   4   5

I am taking a break from _____. I give myself permission to get

back up and start _____ again on/at_____.

Check in to check out: What other emotions or things am I experiencing today?
_____.

My latest self-takeaway: _____.

Reflection: What do I want to remember from the last question I focused on?

_____

_____

_____

_____

_____

_____

_____

6. What do other people say about you? What do you know about yourself? Do these perceptions align with one another? Why or why not?

Set the Mood and Tone for Today's Journaling

Date and Time: _____ Location: _____.

Today my sound choice is: _____.

Smells, if any: _____ Drinking or eating anything: _____.

I am looking at and noticing _____ surrounding me.

Tasks I accomplished today: _____.

How accomplished I feel today: 1   2   3   4   5

I am taking a break from _____. I give myself permission to get back up and start _____ again on/at _____.

Check in to check out: What other emotions or things am I experiencing today?
_____.

My latest self-takeaway: _____.

Reflection: What do I want to remember from the last question I focused on?

_____

_____

_____

_____

_____

_____

_____

Your Journey Begins Here

7. Do you pause often? If not, what do you need to help you remember to do so?

Set the Mood and Tone for Today's Journaling

Date and Time: _____ Location: _____.

Today my sound choice is: _____

Smells, if any: _____ Drinking or eating anything: _____.

I am looking at and noticing _____ surrounding me.

Tasks I accomplished today: _____.

How accomplished I feel today: 1   2   3   4   5

I am taking a break from _____. I give myself permission to get

back up and start _____ again on/at _____.

Check in to check out: What other emotions or things am I experiencing today?
_____.

My latest self-takeaway: _____.

Reflection: What do I want to remember from the last question I focused on?

_____

_____

_____

_____

_____

_____

_____

Your Journey Begins Here

8. Where do you want to be at the end of your therapeutic transformation? What else do you want out of your journey through healing?

Set the Mood and Tone for Today's Journaling

Date and Time: _____   Location: _____.

Today my sound choice is: _____.

Smells, if any: _____ Drinking or eating anything: _____.

I am looking at and noticing _____ surrounding me.

Tasks I accomplished today: _____.

How accomplished I feel today: 1   2   3   4   5

I am taking a break from _____. I give myself permission to get

back up and start _____ again on/at _____.

Check in to check out: What other emotions or things am I experiencing today?
_____.

My latest self-takeaway: _____.

Reflection: What do I want to remember from the last question I focused on?

_____

_____

_____

_____

_____

_____

_____

Your Journey Begins Here

9. What's your greatest fantasy? Allow yourself to go there. Dream bigger than you have ever allowed yourself to dream before. Ask this question as many times as it will take before you permit yourself to dream more significantly than you have ever allowed yourself to dream before.

_____

_____

_____

_____

_____

_____

_____

_____

_____

_____

_____

_____

_____

_____

_____

_____

Set the Mood and Tone for Today's Journaling

Date and Time: _____ Location: _____.

Today my sound choice is: _____

Smells, if any: _____ Drinking or eating anything: _____.

I am looking at and noticing _____ surrounding me.

Tasks I accomplished today: _____.

How accomplished I feel today: 1   2   3   4   5

I am taking a break from _____. I give myself permission to get back up and start _____ again on/at _____.

Check in to check out: What other emotions or things am I experiencing today?
_____.

My latest self-takeaway: _____.

Reflection: What do I want to remember from the last question I focused on?

_____
_____
_____
_____
_____
_____
_____
_____

10. What are three things you like about yourself? Why did you choose these three things? Can you please elaborate on each of the things you listed about yourself? What do you especially like about these three things? How do these three things contribute to your authentic self and voice?

Set the Mood and Tone for Today's Journaling

Date and Time: _____   Location: _____.

Today my sound choice is: _____

Smells, if any: _____ Drinking or eating anything: _____.

I am looking at and noticing _____ surrounding me.

Tasks I accomplished today: _____.

How accomplished I feel today: 1   2   3   4   5

I am taking a break from _____. I give myself permission to get back up and start _____ again on/at _____.

Check in to check out: What other emotions or things am I experiencing today?
_____.

My latest self-takeaway: _____.

Reflection: What do I want to remember from the last question I focused on?

_____

_____

_____

_____

_____

_____

_____

_____

Your Journey Begins Here

11. Are you the love of your life? Have you ever been the love of your own life? Have you ever received a love letter? Or ever desired to receive one? If you wrote a love letter to yourself, what would it say? Write your love letter to yourself below—and write one as often as you desire!

Set the Mood and Tone for Today's Journaling

Date and Time: _____   Location: _____.

Today my sound choice is: _____

Smells, if any: _____ Drinking or eating anything: _____.

I am looking at and noticing _____ surrounding me.

Tasks I accomplished today: _____.

How accomplished I feel today: 1   2   3   4   5

I am taking a break from _____. I give myself permission to get

back up and start _____ again on/at _____.

Check in to check out: What other emotions or things am I experiencing today?
_____.

My latest self-takeaway: _____.

Reflection: What do I want to remember from the last question I focused on?

_____

_____

_____

_____

_____

_____

_____

Your Journey Begins Here

12. What is one thing that people love about you? What is one thing that you would say others appreciate about you? What is one thing that others say you do well? Why is the world better with you in it? What were you born to do? What is easy to love about you?

Set the Mood and Tone for Today's Journaling

Date and Time: _____   Location: _____.

Today my sound choice is: _____.

Smells, if any: _____ Drinking or eating anything: _____.

I am looking at and noticing _____ surrounding me.

Tasks I accomplished today: _____.

How accomplished I feel today: 1   2   3   4   5

I am taking a break from _____. I give myself permission to get

back up and start _____ again on/at _____.

Check in to check out: What other emotions or things am I experiencing today?
_____.

My latest self-takeaway: _____.

Reflection: What do I want to remember from the last question I focused on?

_____

_____

_____

_____

_____

_____

_____

Your Journey Begins Here

13. Check in with yourself to check out of things, thoughts, and tasks you are ready to let go of.
What is beginning to make sense? What are your takeaways from any question you have answered in the beginning section? What are you clear about? What are you challenged by? Check in to check out.

Set the Mood and Tone for Today's Journaling

Date and Time: _____   Location: _____.

Today my sound choice is: _____.

Smells, if any: _____ Drinking or eating anything: _____.

I am looking at and noticing _____ surrounding me.

Tasks I accomplished today: _____.

How accomplished I feel today: 1   2   3   4   5

I am taking a break from _____. I give myself permission to get

back up and start _____ again on/at _____.

Check in to check out: What other emotions or things am I experiencing today?
_____.

My latest self-takeaway: _____.

Reflection: What do I want to remember from the last question I focused on?

_____

_____

_____

_____

_____

_____

_____

Your Journey Begins Here

14. What does life look like for you today? How about tomorrow? Next week? Next month? Next year? Five years from now? Ultimately, what does life look like for you? And, how will you know you have made it? Remember, life happens on the way to where you are going. There may be minor arrival points. How will you celebrate those points? The milestones or goals? How will you make sure you pause or slow down to recognize the growth and the cheers? Small, incremental steps will get you to small successes and, ultimately, to your big monumental successes.

_____

_____

_____

_____

_____

_____

_____

_____

_____

_____

_____

_____

_____

_____

_____

Set the Mood and Tone for Today's Journaling

Date and Time: _____ Location: _____.

Today my sound choice is: _____.

Smells, if any: _____ Drinking or eating anything: _____.

I am looking at and noticing _____ surrounding me.

Tasks I accomplished today: _____.

How accomplished I feel today: 1   2   3   4   5

I am taking a break from _____. I give myself permission to get

back up and start _____ again on/at_____.

Check in to check out: What other emotions or things am I experiencing today?
_____.

My latest self-takeaway: _____.

Reflection: What do I want to remember from the last question I focused on?

_____

_____

_____

_____

_____

_____

_____

Your Journey Begins Here

15. Do you have any other thoughts that need to be shared here? Even if you think you may never walk into a therapist's office, pretend that you are with a therapist right now. What things do you want to make sure to talk about in your journal? What do you want to have clarity about? What do you want to feel good about?

_____
_____
_____
_____
_____
_____
_____
_____
_____
_____
_____
_____
_____
_____
_____
_____

Set the Mood and Tone for Today's Journaling

Date and Time: _____   Location: _____.

Today my sound choice is: _____.

Smells, if any: _____ Drinking or eating anything: _____.

I am looking at and noticing _____ surrounding me.

Tasks I accomplished today: _____.

How accomplished I feel today: 1   2   3   4   5

I am taking a break from _____. I give myself permission to get

back up and start _____ again on/at _____.

Check in to check out: What other emotions or things am I experiencing today?
_____.

My latest self-takeaway: _____.

Reflection: What do I want to remember from the last question I focused on?

_____

_____

_____

_____

_____

_____

_____

Your Journey Begins Here

16. How do you distinguish between being mean and standing up for yourself? What's the difference between the two? How might you tell yourself which category something you have done belongs in? Take any feedback you find helpful and discard the rest.

___
___
___
___
___
___
___
___
___
___
___
___
___
___
___
___

Set the Mood and Tone for Today's Journaling

Date and Time: _____   Location: _____.

Today my sound choice is: _____.

Smells, if any: _____ Drinking or eating anything: _____.

I am looking at and noticing _____ surrounding me.

Tasks I accomplished today: _____.

How accomplished I feel today: 1   2   3   4   5

I am taking a break from _____. I give myself permission to get

back up and start _____ again on/at _____.

Check in to check out: What other emotions or things am I experiencing today?
_____

My latest self-takeaway: _____.

Reflection: What do I want to remember from the last question I focused on?

_____

_____

_____

_____

_____

_____

_____

Your Journey Begins Here

17. What do you currently suffer from? Did you know that suffering is a part of life? That it's a part of the process? I do not mean torture; I mean short-term suffering (and sometimes long-term). The Creator will show you the purpose of your suffering if you are open to it. (If not, I understand. You might not be in that space now.)

_____
_____
_____
_____
_____
_____
_____
_____
_____
_____
_____
_____
_____
_____
_____

Set the Mood and Tone for Today's Journaling

Date and Time: _____   Location: _____.

Today my sound choice is: _____

Smells, if any: _____ Drinking or eating anything: _____.

I am looking at and noticing _____ surrounding me.

Tasks I accomplished today: _____.

How accomplished I feel today: 1   2   3   4   5

I am taking a break from _____. I give myself permission to get

back up and start _____ again on/at _____.

Check in to check out: What other emotions or things am I experiencing today?
_____.

My latest self-takeaway: _____.

Reflection: What do I want to remember from the last question I focused on?

_____

_____

_____

_____

_____

_____

_____

Your Journey Begins Here

18. Do you allow yourself to feel the feels? Or the thrills? What does that look like? Or feel like? What have you processed as a result?

Set the Mood and Tone for Today's Journaling

Date and Time: _____   Location: _____.

Today my sound choice is: _____

Smells, if any: _____ Drinking or eating anything: _____.

I am looking at and noticing _____ surrounding me.

Tasks I accomplished today: _____.

How accomplished I feel today: 1   2   3   4   5

I am taking a break from _____. I give myself permission to get

back up and start _____ again on/at _____.

Check in to check out: What other emotions or things am I experiencing today?
_____.

My latest self-takeaway: _____.

Reflection: What do I want to remember from the last question I focused on?

_____

_____

_____

_____

_____

_____

_____

Your Journey Begins Here

19. What fun things are you doing in your life? These are things you may be doing daily, weekly, monthly, or annually. How do you make sure to keep fun—real fun, not pretend fun—in your life? What's holding you back if you can't answer this question to your satisfaction?

Set the Mood and Tone for Today's Journaling

Date and Time: _____   Location: _____.

Today my sound choice is: _____

Smells, if any: _____ Drinking or eating anything: _____.

I am looking at and noticing _____ surrounding me.

Tasks I accomplished today: _____

How accomplished I feel today: 1   2   3   4   5

I am taking a break from _____. I give myself permission to get

back up and start _____ again on/at_____.

Check in to check out: What other emotions or things am I experiencing today?
_____.

My latest self-takeaway: _____.

Reflection: What do I want to remember from the last question I focused on?

_____

_____

_____

_____

_____

_____

_____

Your Journey Begins Here

20. Have you ever thrown a pity party for yourself? What was the pity party for? In other words, what were you going through that prompted you to feel sorry for yourself? Were you trying to get someone else to feel sorry for you? Consider why you may indulge in self-pity or seek pity from others. What are you looking for? What are you looking to resolve?

_____

_____

_____

_____

_____

_____

_____

_____

_____

_____

_____

_____

_____

_____

_____

_____

21. How much time do you need for your pity parties? Has this decreased over time? (For example, maybe you used to have a pity party for a whole week, but last year you cut that down to one day. Now, you are down to fifteen minutes. That's growth!) If not, what could you do to decrease the amount of time you spend pitying yourself?

_____

Your Journey Begins Here

Set the Mood and Tone for Today's Journaling

Date and Time: _____   Location: _____.

Today my sound choice is: _____.

Smells, if any: _____ Drinking or eating anything: _____.

I am looking at and noticing _____ surrounding me.

Tasks I accomplished today: _____.

How accomplished I feel today: 1   2   3   4   5

I am taking a break from _____. I give myself permission to get back up and start _____ again on/at _____.

Check in to check out: What other emotions or things am I experiencing today?
_____.

My latest self-takeaway: _____.

Reflection: What do I want to remember from the last question I focused on?

_____

_____

_____

_____

_____

_____

_____

_____

22. How much time do you need to adjust after a difficult time? What types of prompts and resources do you need to move through your difficult time? Are you able to give yourself some grace here?

Set the Mood and Tone for Today's Journaling

Date and Time: _____ Location: _____.

Today my sound choice is: _____

Smells, if any: _____ Drinking or eating anything: _____.

I am looking at and noticing _____ surrounding me.

Tasks I accomplished today: _____.

How accomplished I feel today: 1   2   3   4   5

I am taking a break from _____. I give myself permission to get

back up and start _____ again on/at _____.

Check in to check out: What other emotions or things am I experiencing today?
_____.

My latest self-takeaway: _____.

Reflection: What do I want to remember from the last question I focused on?

_____

_____

_____

_____

_____

_____

_____

Your Journey Begins Here

23. How much time do you waste when you think you're being productive? What's eating up your time? Who's eating your time? How do you balance your time and tasks to create a balanced life, day, or moment? Have you ever heard the statement that we are only as busy as we allow ourselves to be? Try doing a time study for one day and then again for one week. Record precisely what you are doing and how much time each task takes. Include personal time and moments of rest.

_____

_____

_____

_____

_____

_____

_____

_____

_____

_____

_____

_____

_____

_____

_____

_____

_____

Set the Mood and Tone for Today's Journaling

Date and Time: _____ Location: _____.

Today my sound choice is: _____.

Smells, if any: _____ Drinking or eating anything: _____.

I am looking at and noticing _____ surrounding me.

Tasks I accomplished today: _____.

How accomplished I feel today: 1   2   3   4   5

I am taking a break from _____. I give myself permission to get

back up and start _____ again on/at _____.

Check in to check out: What other emotions or things am I experiencing today?
_____.

My latest self-takeaway: _____.

Reflection: What do I want to remember from the last question I focused on?

_____

_____

_____

_____

_____

_____

_____

24. What are you avoiding by working too much? Or by taking so many classes? By always being busy? Or by always saying, "I'm busy"?

Set the Mood and Tone for Today's Journaling

Date and Time: _____   Location: _____.

Today my sound choice is: _____

Smells, if any: _____   Drinking or eating anything: _____.

I am looking at and noticing _____ surrounding me.

Tasks I accomplished today: _____.

How accomplished I feel today: 1   2   3   4   5

I am taking a break from _____. I give myself permission to get back up and start _____ again on/at _____.

Check in to check out: What other emotions or things am I experiencing today?
_____.

My latest self-takeaway: _____.

Reflection: What do I want to remember from the last question I focused on?

_____

_____

_____

_____

_____

_____

_____

25. What do you do for pleasure? Do you think you deserve pleasure? Or adult fun? Do you allow yourself to be silly? Or, as other people have called me, goofy? I like to have fun, but as an adult, I sometimes feel like I must suppress my fun self—and I don't enjoy doing that. What about you?

Set the Mood and Tone for Today's Journaling

Date and Time: _____ Location: _____.

Today my sound choice is: _____

Smells, if any: _____ Drinking or eating anything: _____.

I am looking at and noticing _____ surrounding me.

Tasks I accomplished today: _____

How accomplished I feel today: 1   2   3   4   5

I am taking a break from _____. I give myself permission to get

back up and start _____ again on/at _____.

Check in to check out: What other emotions or things am I experiencing today?
_____.

My latest self-takeaway: _____.

Reflection: What do I want to remember from the last question I focused on?

_____

_____

_____

_____

_____

_____

_____

Your Journey Begins Here

Pause Moment #3

You do not have to suffer alone.

**It is okay to ask for
and receive support.
You have people,
you just have to identify them.**

Whoosah! Take a deep breath and embrace new beginnings. Simplify your breathing—it can be easy. Breathe deeply and let out a sigh of relief. Allow yourself to be flexible with your breathing. Inhale through your nose, exhale through your mouth. Feel your chest rise and fall with each breath. Keep breathing until you've taken in all the air you need.

A better vibe, A better life

Set the Mood and Tone for Today's Journaling

Date and Time: _____   Location: _____.

Today my sound choice is: _____.

Smells, if any: _____ Drinking or eating anything: _____.

I am looking at and noticing _____ surrounding me.

Tasks I accomplished today: _____.

How accomplished I feel today: 1   2   3   4   5

I am taking a break from _____. I give myself permission to get

back up and start _____ again on/at _____.

Check in to check out: What other emotions or things am I experiencing today?
_____.

My latest self-takeaway: _____.

Reflection: What do I want to remember from the last question I focused on?

_____

_____

_____

_____

_____

_____

_____

A Better Vibe, a Better Life

26. What trust issues can you identify? As you identify those trust issues, can you also explore them? Where did they come from? Whom did they come from? Go as deep as you can during this identification and discovery task. Do you think it is possible to trust again? If so, what will it take? What do you specifically need to trust again, and from whom?

_____
_____
_____
_____
_____
_____
_____
_____
_____
_____
_____
_____
_____
_____
_____
_____

Set the Mood and Tone for Today's Journaling

Date and Time: _____ Location: _____.

Today my sound choice is: _____.

Smells, if any: _____ Drinking or eating anything: _____.

I am looking at and noticing _____ surrounding me.

Tasks I accomplished today: _____.

How accomplished I feel today:　　1　　2　　3　　4　　5

I am taking a break from _____. I give myself permission to get back up and start _____ again on/at _____.

Check in to check out: What other emotions or things am I experiencing today?
_____.

My latest self-takeaway: _____.

Reflection: What do I want to remember from the last question I focused on?

_____

_____

_____

_____

_____

_____

_____

A Better Vibe, a Better Life

27. Do you feel included? Like you belong? Do you feel included and like you belong everywhere you go? Give an example of a place where you have felt included. Give another example of a place where you have felt excluded.

Set the Mood and Tone for Today's Journaling

Date and Time: _____   Location: _____.

Today my sound choice is: _____.

Smells, if any: _____   Drinking or eating anything: _____.

I am looking at and noticing _____ surrounding me.

Tasks I accomplished today: _____.

How accomplished I feel today: 1   2   3   4   5

I am taking a break from _____. I give myself permission to get

back up and start _____ again on/at _____.

Check in to check out: What other emotions or things am I experiencing today?
_____.

My latest self-takeaway: _____.

Reflection: What do I want to remember from the last question I focused on?

_____

_____

_____

_____

_____

_____

_____

A Better Vibe, a Better Life

28. How do you love yourself? What do you need to love yourself?

   a. Has anyone ever shown you how to love? If so, who?

   b. Have you ever felt loved? If so, what did that feel like?

   c. How do you keep that feeling of being loved going? How do you replicate it?

   d. Do you expect others to show you how to love or be loved?

   e. Are you tired of people telling you to love yourself before you love others (or before you can expect others to love you)?

Set the Mood and Tone for Today's Journaling

Date and Time: _____ Location: _____.

Today my sound choice is: _____.

Smells, if any: _____ Drinking or eating anything: _____.

I am looking at and noticing _____ surrounding me.

Tasks I accomplished today: _____.

How accomplished I feel today: 1   2   3   4   5

I am taking a break from _____. I give myself permission to get

back up and start _____ again on/at _____.

Check in to check out: What other emotions or things am I experiencing today?
_____.

My latest self-takeaway: _____.

Reflection: What do I want to remember from the last question I focused on?

_____

_____

_____

_____

_____

_____

_____

_____

A Better Vibe, a Better Life

29. What have you been close to? Sometimes in life, you may have felt like there were times when you were close to something meaningful, but never really reached the point of completion, contention, or satisfaction. What have you been closed off from? What are you now open to?

Set the Mood and Tone for Today's Journaling

Date and Time: _____   Location: _____.

Today my sound choice is: _____

Smells, if any: _____ Drinking or eating anything: _____.

I am looking at and noticing _____ surrounding me.

Tasks I accomplished today: _____.

How accomplished I feel today: 1   2   3   4   5

I am taking a break from _____. I give myself permission to get

back up and start _____ again on/at _____.

Check in to check out: What other emotions or things am I experiencing today?
_____.

My latest self-takeaway: _____.

Reflection: What do I want to remember from the last question I focused on?

_____

_____

_____

_____

_____

_____

_____

A Better Vibe, a Better Life

30. What trust issues stem from your upbringing? What familial trust issues were present during your childhood experience?

Set the Mood and Tone for Today's Journaling

Date and Time: _____ Location: _____.

Today my sound choice is: _____

Smells, if any: _____ Drinking or eating anything: _____.

I am looking at and noticing _____ surrounding me.

Tasks I accomplished today: _____.

How accomplished I feel today: 1   2   3   4   5

I am taking a break from _____. I give myself permission to get back up and start _____ again on/at _____.

Check in to check out: What other emotions or things am I experiencing today?
_____.

My latest self-takeaway: _____.

Reflection: What do I want to remember from the last question I focused on?

_____
_____
_____
_____
_____
_____
_____
_____

31. What are some of your biases? What are other people's biases toward you? Implicit and explicit biases are two examples of such biases to think about for this question. Implicit bias lives inside your body and mind. For example, without thought, you prejudge a person based on what you think you know about that person and their culture or group. Explicit biases are acts of outwardly and knowingly prejudging another without regard to how they might be impacted.

_____
_____
_____
_____
_____
_____
_____
_____
_____
_____
_____
_____
_____
_____
_____

Set the Mood and Tone for Today's Journaling

Date and Time: _____   Location: _____.

Today my sound choice is: _____

Smells, if any: _____ Drinking or eating anything: _____.

I am looking at and noticing _____ surrounding me.

Tasks I accomplished today: _____.

How accomplished I feel today: 1   2   3   4   5

I am taking a break from _____. I give myself permission to get back up and start _____ again on/at _____.

Check in to check out: What other emotions or things am I experiencing today?
_____.

My latest self-takeaway: _____.

Reflection: What do I want to remember from the last question I focused on?

_____

_____

_____

_____

_____

_____

_____

A Better Vibe, a Better Life

32. Have you ever been in a situation where you felt "less than" and not treated equally? What contributed to you feeling that way? What did you do about it? Is that something you can use to move forward through similar situations in the future?

_____
_____
_____
_____
_____
_____
_____
_____
_____
_____
_____
_____
_____
_____
_____
_____
_____
_____

Set the Mood and Tone for Today's Journaling

Date and Time: _____ Location: _____.

Today my sound choice is: _____.

Smells, if any: _____ Drinking or eating anything: _____.

I am looking at and noticing _____ surrounding me.

Tasks I accomplished today: _____.

How accomplished I feel today: 1   2   3   4   5

I am taking a break from _____. I give myself permission to get back up and start _____ again on/at _____.

Check in to check out: What other emotions or things am I experiencing today?
_____.

My latest self-takeaway: _____.

Reflection: What do I want to remember from the last question I focused on?

_____

_____

_____

_____

_____

_____

_____

_____

A Better Vibe, a Better Life

33. How can you make sure that you matter? To yourself? In situations with other people? What can you do when you find yourself feeling less than outstanding?

Set the Mood and Tone for Today's Journaling

Date and Time: _____   Location: _____.

Today my sound choice is: _____

Smells, if any: _____ Drinking or eating anything: _____.

I am looking at and noticing _____ surrounding me.

Tasks I accomplished today: _____.

How accomplished I feel today: 1   2   3   4   5

I am taking a break from _____. I give myself permission to get

back up and start _____ again on/at _____.

Check in to check out: What other emotions or things am I experiencing today?
_____

My latest self-takeaway: _____.

Reflection: What do I want to remember from the last question I focused on?

_____

_____

_____

_____

_____

_____

_____

A Better Vibe, a Better Life

34. How do you embrace change? What holds you back from doing so? What are you afraid of when it comes to change? What is exciting about change? Why do you feel this way about it? Have you ever explored these reasons?

_____
_____
_____
_____
_____
_____
_____
_____
_____
_____
_____
_____
_____
_____
_____
_____
_____

Set the Mood and Tone for Today's Journaling

Date and Time: _____   Location: _____.

Today my sound choice is: _____.

Smells, if any: _____ Drinking or eating anything: _____.

I am looking at and noticing _____ surrounding me.

Tasks I accomplished today: _____.

How accomplished I feel today: 1   2   3   4   5

I am taking a break from _____. I give myself permission to get

back up and start _____ again on/at _____.

Check in to check out: What other emotions or things am I experiencing today?
_____.

My latest self-takeaway: _____.

Reflection: What do I want to remember from the last question I focused on?

_____

_____

_____

_____

_____

_____

_____

A Better Vibe, a Better Life

35. What inspires you? And, what does not inspire you? How do you know this? What tells you that something does or doesn't inspire you?

Set the Mood and Tone for Today's Journaling

Date and Time: _____   Location: _____.

Today my sound choice is: _____

Smells, if any: _____ Drinking or eating anything: _____.

I am looking at and noticing _____ surrounding me.

Tasks I accomplished today: _____.

How accomplished I feel today: 1   2   3   4   5

I am taking a break from _____. I give myself permission to get

back up and start _____ again on/at _____.

Check in to check out: What other emotions or things am I experiencing today?
_____

My latest self-takeaway: _____.

Reflection: What do I want to remember from the last question I focused on?

_____

_____

_____

_____

_____

_____

_____

A Better Vibe, a Better Life

36. What kind of people do you attract? What type of energy or behaviors do you attract? What do you want to stop attracting? Be honest with yourself, or you will never get what you desire.

Set the Mood and Tone for Today's Journaling

Date and Time: _____ Location: _____.

Today my sound choice is: _____.

Smells, if any: _____ Drinking or eating anything: _____.

I am looking at and noticing _____ surrounding me.

Tasks I accomplished today: _____.

How accomplished I feel today: 1   2   3   4   5

I am taking a break from _____. I give myself permission to get

back up and start _____ again on/at _____.

Check in to check out: What other emotions or things am I experiencing today?
_____.

My latest self-takeaway: _____.

Reflection: What do I want to remember from the last question I focused on?

_____

_____

_____

_____

_____

_____

_____

37. What are your deepest desires? Will you allow yourself to go there? If not, what are you afraid of?

Set the Mood and Tone for Today's Journaling

Date and Time: _____ Location: _____.

Today my sound choice is: _____.

Smells, if any: _____ Drinking or eating anything: _____.

I am looking at and noticing _____ surrounding me.

Tasks I accomplished today: _____.

How accomplished I feel today: 1   2   3   4   5

I am taking a break from _____. I give myself permission to get

back up and start _____ again on/at _____.

Check in to check out: What other emotions or things am I experiencing today?
_____.

My latest self-takeaway: _____.

Reflection: What do I want to remember from the last question I focused on?

_____

_____

_____

_____

_____

_____

_____

A Better Vibe, a Better Life

38. What excites you? What touches the deepest, most sultry part of your body?

Set the Mood and Tone for Today's Journaling

Date and Time: _____ Location: _____.

Today my sound choice is: _____

Smells, if any: _____ Drinking or eating anything: _____.

I am looking at and noticing _____ surrounding me.

Tasks I accomplished today: _____.

How accomplished I feel today: 1   2   3   4   5

I am taking a break from _____. I give myself permission to get

back up and start _____ again on/at _____.

Check in to check out: What other emotions or things am I experiencing today?
_____.

My latest self-takeaway: _____.

Reflection: What do I want to remember from the last question I focused on?

_____

_____

_____

_____

_____

_____

_____

39. What do you dream of? Dream big and bold.

Set the Mood and Tone for Today's Journaling

Date and Time: _____   Location: _____.

Today my sound choice is: _____

Smells, if any: _____ Drinking or eating anything: _____.

I am looking at and noticing _____ surrounding me.

Tasks I accomplished today: _____.

How accomplished I feel today: 1   2   3   4   5

I am taking a break from _____. I give myself permission to get

back up and start _____ again on/at _____.

Check in to check out: What other emotions or things am I experiencing today?
_____.

My latest self-takeaway: _____.

Reflection: What do I want to remember from the last question I focused on?

_____

_____

_____

_____

_____

_____

_____

_____

40. What are you holding out hope for? In your life? For example, what did you expect your life to be like? What do you expect your life to be like now?

Set the Mood and Tone for Today's Journaling

Date and Time: _____   Location: _____.

Today my sound choice is: _____

Smells, if any: _____ Drinking or eating anything: _____.

I am looking at and noticing _____ surrounding me.

Tasks I accomplished today: _____.

How accomplished I feel today: 1   2   3   4   5

I am taking a break from _____. I give myself permission to get

back up and start _____ again on/at _____.

Check in to check out: What other emotions or things am I experiencing today?
_____.

My latest self-takeaway: _____.

Reflection: What do I want to remember from the last question I focused on?

_____

_____

_____

_____

_____

_____

_____

A Better Vibe, a Better Life

41. What do you need to move away from? What's keeping you stuck? Why does it have so much power? Who is keeping you stuck? Why do they have so much power?

Set the Mood and Tone for Today's Journaling

Date and Time: _____ Location: _____.

Today my sound choice is: _____.

Smells, if any: _____ Drinking or eating anything: _____.

I am looking at and noticing _____ surrounding me.

Tasks I accomplished today: _____.

How accomplished I feel today: 1   2   3   4   5

I am taking a break from _____. I give myself permission to get back up and start _____ again on/at _____.

Check in to check out: What other emotions or things am I experiencing today?
_____.

My latest self-takeaway: _____.

Reflection: What do I want to remember from the last question I focused on?

_____

_____

_____

_____

_____

_____

_____

A Better Vibe, a Better Life

42. Do you think you can keep moving while feeling stuck? What do you need so you can move forward?

Set the Mood and Tone for Today's Journaling

Date and Time: _____ Location: _____.

Today my sound choice is: _____

Smells, if any: _____ Drinking or eating anything: _____.

I am looking at and noticing _____ surrounding me.

Tasks I accomplished today: _____.

How accomplished I feel today: 1   2   3   4   5

I am taking a break from _____. I give myself permission to get back up and start _____ again on/at _____.

Check in to check out: What other emotions or things am I experiencing today?
_____.

My latest self-takeaway: _____.

Reflection: What do I want to remember from the last question I focused on?

_____

_____

_____

_____

_____

_____

_____

43. What is holding you back? Is it yourself? Or somebody else? How do you know? How can you confirm this for yourself right now?

Set the Mood and Tone for Today's Journaling

Date and Time: _____ Location: _____.

Today my sound choice is: _____

Smells, if any: _____ Drinking or eating anything: _____.

I am looking at and noticing _____ surrounding me.

Tasks I accomplished today: _____.

How accomplished I feel today: 1   2   3   4   5

I am taking a break from _____. I give myself permission to get

back up and start _____ again on/at _____.

Check in to check out: What other emotions or things am I experiencing today?
_____.

My latest self-takeaway: _____.

Reflection: What do I want to remember from the last question I focused on?

_____

_____

_____

_____

_____

_____

_____

A Better Vibe, a Better Life

44. What's your driving force in life? What will continue to drive you? What doesn't drive you and keeps you stuck instead?

Set the Mood and Tone for Today's Journaling

Date and Time: _____   Location: _____.

Today my sound choice is: _____.

Smells, if any: _____ Drinking or eating anything: _____.

I am looking at and noticing _____ surrounding me.

Tasks I accomplished today: _____.

How accomplished I feel today: 1   2   3   4   5

I am taking a break from _____. I give myself permission to get

back up and start _____ again on/at _____.

Check in to check out: What other emotions or things am I experiencing today?
_____.

My latest self-takeaway: _____.

Reflection: What do I want to remember from the last question I focused on?

_____

_____

_____

_____

_____

_____

_____

_____

A Better Vibe, a Better Life

45. What binds you? In a good way? Or in a bad way? What are things that feel binding? What keeps you strongly held to something? Do you ever feel restrained? In what ways have you felt loosed by something confining or binding?

Set the Mood and Tone for Today's Journaling

Date and Time: _____   Location: _____.

Today my sound choice is: _____.

Smells, if any: _____ Drinking or eating anything: _____.

I am looking at and noticing _____ surrounding me.

Tasks I accomplished today: _____.

How accomplished I feel today: 1   2   3   4   5

I am taking a break from _____. I give myself permission to get

back up and start _____ again on/at _____.

Check in to check out: What other emotions or things am I experiencing today?
_____.

My latest self-takeaway: _____.

Reflection: What do I want to remember from the last question I focused on?

_____

_____

_____

_____

_____

_____

_____

46. What are you breathing through? What's making you gasp for air, literally and figuratively?

Set the Mood and Tone for Today's Journaling

Date and Time: _____   Location: _____.

Today my sound choice is: _____

Smells, if any: _____ Drinking or eating anything: _____.

I am looking at and noticing _____ surrounding me.

Tasks I accomplished today: _____.

How accomplished I feel today: 1   2   3   4   5

I am taking a break from _____. I give myself permission to get

back up and start _____ again on/at _____.

Check in to check out: What other emotions or things am I experiencing today?
_____.

My latest self-takeaway: _____.

Reflection: What do I want to remember from the last question I focused on?

_____

_____

_____

_____

_____

_____

_____

A Better Vibe, a Better Life

47. What makes you want to fight? What are you willing to stand up to? What have you had to fight for in your life? What or who are you willing to stand up to?

Set the Mood and Tone for Today's Journaling

Date and Time: _____ Location: _____.

Today my sound choice is: _____.

Smells, if any: _____ Drinking or eating anything: _____.

I am looking at and noticing _____ surrounding me.

Tasks I accomplished today: _____.

How accomplished I feel today: 1   2   3   4   5

I am taking a break from _____. I give myself permission to get back up and start _____ again on/at _____.

Check in to check out: What other emotions or things am I experiencing today?
_____.

My latest self-takeaway: _____.

Reflection: What do I want to remember from the last question I focused on?

_____

_____

_____

_____

_____

_____

_____

48. What makes you want to flee? What makes you want to run? What have you been running from all of your life? What are you currently fleeing from?

_____
_____
_____
_____
_____
_____
_____
_____
_____
_____
_____
_____
_____
_____
_____
_____

Set the Mood and Tone for Today's Journaling

Date and Time: _____ Location: _____.

Today my sound choice is: _____

Smells, if any: _____ Drinking or eating anything: _____.

I am looking at and noticing _____ surrounding me.

Tasks I accomplished today: _____.

How accomplished I feel today: 1   2   3   4   5

I am taking a break from _____. I give myself permission to get

back up and start _____ again on/at _____.

Check in to check out: What other emotions or things am I experiencing today?
_____.

My latest self-takeaway: _____.

Reflection: What do I want to remember from the last question I focused on?

_____

_____

_____

_____

_____

_____

_____

A Better Vibe, a Better Life

49. What's making you freeze right now? What shocks you? What stops you? What keeps you stuck in a place or position you don't want to be in?

Set the Mood and Tone for Today's Journaling

Date and Time: _____ Location: _____.

Today my sound choice is: _____.

Smells, if any: _____ Drinking or eating anything: _____.

I am looking at and noticing _____ surrounding me.

Tasks I accomplished today: _____.

How accomplished I feel today: 1   2   3   4   5

I am taking a break from _____. I give myself permission to get back up and start _____ again on/at _____.

Check in to check out: What other emotions or things am I experiencing today?
_____.

My latest self-takeaway: _____.

Reflection: What do I want to remember from the last question I focused on?

_____

_____

_____

_____

_____

_____

A Better Vibe, a Better Life

50. What makes you flow? What makes you feel like you are floating on air or in midspace? What makes you feel free and floaty inside? What tells you that you are flowing in everyday tasks, projects, and life? What activities do you flow into? What areas do you wish you could flow in?

Set the Mood and Tone for Today's Journaling

Date and Time: _____   Location: _____.

Today my sound choice is: _____.

Smells, if any: _____   Drinking or eating anything: _____.

I am looking at and noticing _____ surrounding me.

Tasks I accomplished today: _____.

How accomplished I feel today: 1   2   3   4   5

I am taking a break from _____. I give myself permission to get

back up and start _____ again on/at _____.

Check in to check out: What other emotions or things am I experiencing today?
_____.

My latest self-takeaway: _____.

Reflection: What do I want to remember from the last question I focused on?

_____

_____

_____

_____

_____

_____

A Better Vibe, a Better Life

Pause Moment #4

You are worth it.

**You are valuable
and important.
Your existence matters.**

Take a moment to pause and breathe. Exhale a sigh of relief and inhale a deep breath of gratitude for your healing journey.

Continue to breathe in and out until you find your rhythm. Bring your awareness to your breathing. How does it feel? Is it fast or slow? Take note of your breathing pattern and become familiar with it. Now, put your hand on your chest and feel the rise and fall of your chest. Sit inside this breathing pattern and rhythm until you become calm, relaxed, and satisfied. Sit inside it until you feel one with your breath. Ahhhhh.

Gathering to grow

Set the Mood and Tone for Today's Journaling

Date and Time: _____ Location: _____.

Today my sound choice is: _____.

Smells, if any: _____ Drinking or eating anything: _____.

I am looking at and noticing _____ surrounding me.

Tasks I accomplished today: _____.

How accomplished I feel today: 1   2   3   4   5

I am taking a break from _____. I give myself permission to get

back up and start _____ again on/at _____.

Check in to check out: What other emotions or things am I experiencing today?
_____.

My latest self-takeaway: _____.

Reflection: What do I want to remember from the last question I focused on?

_____

_____

_____

_____

_____

_____

_____

51. Who are you as a person, friend, or family member? Do you like who you are right now? And, who are you in comparison to who you were yesterday and before that? This prompt encourages you to think about different angles of this question, such as: How have you changed?

    a. Was that change intentional?
    b. How can you change if you desire change?
    c. Do you trust yourself? Remember, trust yourself—and trust the process!
    d. What does change look like?
    e. What are you afraid of?
    f. What are you excited about?
    g. What empowers you?
    h. How can you maintain what's working?
    i. How can you discard what's not working?
    j. How can you bask in the unknown?
    k. Are you ever in your own way? You can think about this question in these ways:

        i. Your goals
        ii. Dating, relationships, and/or family connections
        iii. Career, work, and/or educational journey
        iv. Socializing and/or leisure
        v. Your passions
        vi. Spirituality
        vii. Your physical growth and your physical body
        viii. Your mental state and your mental growth
        ix. Forgiving yourself, forgiving other people, and forgiving circumstances
        x. Physical movement and moving forward
        xi. Your personal growth and your growth as a result of changes
        xii. Your desires and/or "fires"
        xiii. Bettering yourself

Gathering to Grow

Set the Mood and Tone for Today's Journaling

Date and Time: _____   Location: _____.

Today my sound choice is: _____

Smells, if any: _____ Drinking or eating anything: _____.

I am looking at and noticing _____ surrounding me.

Tasks I accomplished today: _____.

How accomplished I feel today: 1   2   3   4   5

I am taking a break from _____. I give myself permission to get back up and start _____ again on/at _____.

Check in to check out: What other emotions or things am I experiencing today?
_____.

My latest self-takeaway: _____.

Reflection: What do I want to remember from the last question I focused on?

_____
_____
_____
_____
_____
_____
_____

52. What fills your cup? What empties your cup? If certain people are emptying your cup, call them out below so you can know for sure. You have to know to grow.

Set the Mood and Tone for Today's Journaling

Date and Time: _____ Location: _____.

Today my sound choice is: _____

Smells, if any: _____ Drinking or eating anything: _____.

I am looking at and noticing _____ surrounding me.

Tasks I accomplished today: _____.

How accomplished I feel today: 1   2   3   4   5

I am taking a break from _____. I give myself permission to get back up and start _____ again on/at _____.

Check in to check out: What other emotions or things am I experiencing today?
_____.

My latest self-takeaway: _____.

Reflection: What do I want to remember from the last question I focused on?

_____

_____

_____

_____

_____

_____

53. What do you need to grow? What's killing your growth vibe? Did you know that with growth comes increasing pain (i.e., growing pains)?

Set the Mood and Tone for Today's Journaling

Date and Time: _____ Location: _____.

Today my sound choice is: _____

Smells, if any: _____ Drinking or eating anything: _____.

I am looking at and noticing _____ surrounding me.

Tasks I accomplished today: _____.

How accomplished I feel today: 1   2   3   4   5

I am taking a break from _____. I give myself permission to get back up and start _____ again on/at _____.

Check in to check out: What other emotions or things am I experiencing today?
_____

My latest self-takeaway: _____.

Reflection: What do I want to remember from the last question I focused on?

_____

_____

_____

_____

_____

_____

_____

Gathering to Grow

54. What are your current growing pains? Or your current strains?

55. What is the best advice somebody has given you about development or growing pains?

Set the Mood and Tone for Today's Journaling

Date and Time: _____ Location: _____.

Today my sound choice is: _____

Smells, if any: _____ Drinking or eating anything: _____.

I am looking at and noticing _____ surrounding me.

Tasks I accomplished today: _____.

How accomplished I feel today: 1   2   3   4   5

I am taking a break from _____. I give myself permission to get

back up and start _____ again on/at _____.

Check in to check out: What other emotions or things am I experiencing today?
_____.

My latest self-takeaway: _____.

Reflection: What do I want to remember from the last question I focused on?

_____

_____

_____

_____

_____

_____

_____

56. What growing pains are you experiencing from your last growth spurt? You are here to tell the story. How can you use this story to plant future seeds of courage for growth? Keep growing so you can keep glowing.

Set the Mood and Tone for Today's Journaling

Date and Time: _____ Location: _____.

Today my sound choice is: _____

Smells, if any: _____ Drinking or eating anything: _____.

I am looking at and noticing _____ surrounding me.

Tasks I accomplished today: _____.

How accomplished I feel today: 1   2   3   4   5

I am taking a break from _____. I give myself permission to get

back up and start _____ again on/at _____.

Check in to check out: What other emotions or things am I experiencing today?
_____.

My latest self-takeaway: _____.

Reflection: What do I want to remember from the last question I focused on?

_____

_____

_____

_____

_____

_____

_____

57. What will be your legacy from your growth process? What do you want to pass on to others? Remember, somebody is waiting for those jewels or seeds. As you are watching others through your aspirations, somebody is watching you through theirs. Grow tall, not small.

Set the Mood and Tone for Today's Journaling

Date and Time: _____   Location: _____.

Today my sound choice is: _____.

Smells, if any: _____ Drinking or eating anything: _____.

I am looking at and noticing _____ surrounding me.

Tasks I accomplished today: _____.

How accomplished I feel today: 1   2   3   4   5

I am taking a break from _____. I give myself permission to get

back up and start _____ again on/at _____.

Check in to check out: What other emotions or things am I experiencing today?
_____.

My latest self-takeaway: _____.

Reflection: What do I want to remember from the last question I focused on?

_____

_____

_____

_____

_____

_____

_____

58. What do you trust? Who do you trust? What tells you that you can trust something or someone? Were you raised in a trusting environment? Say more.

Set the Mood and Tone for Today's Journaling

Date and Time: _____ Location: _____.

Today my sound choice is: _____

Smells, if any: _____ Drinking or eating anything: _____.

I am looking at and noticing _____ surrounding me.

Tasks I accomplished today: _____.

How accomplished I feel today: 1   2   3   4   5

I am taking a break from _____. I give myself permission to get back up and start _____ again on/at _____.

Check in to check out: What other emotions or things am I experiencing today?
_____.

My latest self-takeaway: _____.

Reflection: What do I want to remember from the last question I focused on?

_____

_____

_____

_____

_____

_____

_____

Gathering to Grow

59. What are you breathing in? And out? What good things will you breathe in? What bad or negative thing will you release or breathe out? (Example: I am breathing in healing, and I am breathing out past trauma/drama.)

Set the Mood and Tone for Today's Journaling

Date and Time: _____   Location: _____.

Today my sound choice is: _____

Smells, if any: _____   Drinking or eating anything: _____.

I am looking at and noticing _____ surrounding me.

Tasks I accomplished today: _____.

How accomplished I feel today: 1   2   3   4   5

I am taking a break from _____. I give myself permission to get back up and start _____ again on/at _____.

Check in to check out: What other emotions or things am I experiencing today?
_____.

My latest self-takeaway: _____.

Reflection: What do I want to remember from the last question I focused on?

_____

_____

_____

_____

_____

_____

_____

60. If you could have three wishes, what would they be? Why these three? Would these wishes change over time? Would you allow for a different response here without guilt, hesitation, or apology? If so, what would your new wishes be?

Set the Mood and Tone for Today's Journaling

Date and Time: _____   Location: _____.

Today my sound choice is: _____.

Smells, if any: _____ Drinking or eating anything: _____.

I am looking at and noticing _____ surrounding me.

Tasks I accomplished today: _____.

How accomplished I feel today: 1   2   3   4   5

I am taking a break from _____. I give myself permission to get

back up and start _____ again on/at _____.

Check in to check out: What other emotions or things am I experiencing today?
_____.

My latest self-takeaway: _____.

Reflection: What do I want to remember from the last question I focused on?

_____

_____

_____

_____

_____

_____

_____

61. What type of support do you need? What does this look like to you? Is it hard to ask for this kind of support when you need it?

62. What type of support do you have? Name people you would consider supportive in your life. How are they supportive, meaning how do they actively or passively show up for you? If you identify as having support, do you know how to use it? *This is your healing village or crew.*

Set the Mood and Tone for Today's Journaling

Date and Time: _____   Location: _____.

Today my sound choice is: _____.

Smells, if any: _____   Drinking or eating anything: _____.

I am looking at and noticing _____ surrounding me.

Tasks I accomplished today: _____.

How accomplished I feel today: 1   2   3   4   5

I am taking a break from _____. I give myself permission to get

back up and start _____ again on/at _____.

Check in to check out: What other emotions or things am I experiencing today?

_____.

My latest self-takeaway: _____.

Reflection: What do I want to remember from the last question I focused on?

_____

_____

_____

_____

_____

_____

_____

63. How do you tell people what you need? Do you do it assertively? Or passively? Do you think they ought to know what you need? Or do you give them hints?

Set the Mood and Tone for Today's Journaling

Date and Time: _____   Location: _____.

Today my sound choice is: _____

Smells, if any: _____   Drinking or eating anything: _____.

I am looking at and noticing _____ surrounding me.

Tasks I accomplished today: _____.

How accomplished I feel today: 1   2   3   4   5

I am taking a break from _____. I give myself permission to get

back up and start _____ again on/at _____.

Check in to check out: What other emotions or things am I experiencing today?
_____.

My latest self-takeaway: _____.

Reflection: What do I want to remember from the last question I focused on?

_____

_____

_____

_____

_____

_____

_____

64. Where is your village or crew? Who is part of it? What else do you need? Who else do you need? Please refer to questions 61 and 62 for additional motivation to answer this question.

65. Do you ask for help? If so, how does it feel to ask for help? What drives you to do so? Also, how does it feel to not ask for help? And what stops you from asking for it?

Set the Mood and Tone for Today's Journaling

Date and Time: _____   Location: _____.

Today my sound choice is: _____

Smells, if any: _____   Drinking or eating anything: _____.

I am looking at and noticing _____ surrounding me.

Tasks I accomplished today: _____.

How accomplished I feel today: 1   2   3   4   5

I am taking a break from _____. I give myself permission to get

back up and start _____ again on/at _____.

Check in to check out: What other emotions or things am I experiencing today?
_____.

My latest self-takeaway: _____.

Reflection: What do I want to remember from the last question I focused on?

_____

_____

_____

_____

_____

_____

_____

_____

66. Who's holding you while you hold others (and while you "hold it down")? If this is a tough question to think about in the moment, go back to questions 64 and 65 to connect with your healing village.

Set the Mood and Tone for Today's Journaling

Date and Time: _____ Location: _____.

Today my sound choice is: _____

Smells, if any: _____ Drinking or eating anything: _____.

I am looking at and noticing _____ surrounding me.

Tasks I accomplished today: _____.

How accomplished I feel today: 1   2   3   4   5

I am taking a break from _____. I give myself permission to get

back up and start _____ again on/at _____.

Check in to check out: What other emotions or things am I experiencing today?
_____.

My latest self-takeaway: _____.

Reflection: What do I want to remember from the last question I focused on?

_____

_____

_____

_____

_____

_____

_____

67. Do you have a perfect partner in mind? Are you the ideal partner? Explain why or why not for both questions.

Set the Mood and Tone for Today's Journaling

Date and Time: _____ Location: _____.

Today my sound choice is: _____

Smells, if any: _____ Drinking or eating anything: _____.

I am looking at and noticing _____ surrounding me.

Tasks I accomplished today: _____.

How accomplished I feel today: 1   2   3   4   5

I am taking a break from _____. I give myself permission to get

back up and start _____ again on/at _____.

Check in to check out: What other emotions or things am I experiencing today?
_____.

My latest self-takeaway: _____.

Reflection: What do I want to remember from the last question I focused on?

_____

_____

_____

_____

_____

_____

_____

68. Who is your personal or intimate thought partner? And who is your professional thought partner?

69. Who motivates you? And, who does not motivate you?

Gathering to Grow

Set the Mood and Tone for Today's Journaling

Date and Time: _____   Location: _____.

Today my sound choice is: _____

Smells, if any: _____ Drinking or eating anything: _____.

I am looking at and noticing _____ surrounding me.

Tasks I accomplished today: _____.

How accomplished I feel today: 1   2   3   4   5

I am taking a break from _____. I give myself permission to get

back up and start _____ again on/at _____.

Check in to check out: What other emotions or things am I experiencing today?
_____.

My latest self-takeaway: _____.

Reflection: What do I want to remember from the last question I focused on?

_____

_____

_____

_____

_____

_____

_____

70. Have you ever been diagnosed with a mental illness? If so, what is it? In your own words, what does this diagnosis mean to you? How do you understand your mental illness and symptoms? Do you agree with the diagnosis? If you disagree with it, what do you think the diagnosis should be? Share what you know about the diagnosis that you think it should be. Do you think a health provider missed something about you? If so, what is it and how do you feel about it?

If none of the above resonates, feel free to share any other interesting thoughts or experiences that come to mind!

71. Have you ever diagnosed yourself with a mental illness? If so, what made you come to the conclusion you did? What tells you that you have a mental illness?

If none of the above resonates, feel free to share any other interesting thoughts or experiences that come to mind!

72. Do you know the difference between mental health and mental illness? Can you define mental health and mental illness in your own words?

If none of the above resonates, feel free to share any other interesting thoughts or experiences that come to mind!

73. Do you have any family members or friends who have been diagnosed with a mental illness?
If so, how does that make you feel? How do you relate it to your mental health experiences?

If none of the above resonates, feel free to share any other interesting thoughts or experiences that come to mind!

74. What are your current thoughts? Or your most recent thoughts?

75. When you think about the answers to the previous questions, where are you emotionally as you experience these thoughts?

Pause Moment #5

Keep going.

As you embark on your healing journey, remember that this is just one piece of the puzzle that will help you establish and maintain the right tone for continuous growth and development.

It's important to take some time to check in with yourself and observe your breathing pattern. You can close your eyes or focus on something calming. Take a moment to notice if your breath is fast or slow, and just simply take a pause and become aware of your breathing.

Healing the narrative

Set the Mood and Tone for Today's Journaling

Date and Time: _____   Location: _____.

Today my sound choice is: _____

Smells, if any: _____   Drinking or eating anything: _____.

I am looking at and noticing _____ surrounding me.

Tasks I accomplished today: _____.

How accomplished I feel today: 1   2   3   4   5

I am taking a break from _____. I give myself permission to get

back up and start _____ again on/at _____.

Check in to check out: What other emotions or things am I experiencing today?
_____.

My latest self-takeaway: _____.

Reflection: What do I want to remember from the last question I focused on?

_____

_____

_____

_____

_____

_____

Healing the Narrative

76. What are you going through right now that is causing you pain? Please dig deeper here if you can. Where are you stuck? What are you going through right now that's asking you to grow and change? What are you moving through? What are you breaking through? And what's breaking through to you?

Set the Mood and Tone for Today's Journaling

Date and Time: _____   Location: _____.

Today my sound choice is: _____

Smells, if any: _____ Drinking or eating anything: _____.

I am looking at and noticing _____ surrounding me.

Tasks I accomplished today: _____.

How accomplished I feel today: 1   2   3   4   5

I am taking a break from _____. I give myself permission to get

back up and start _____ again on/at _____.

Check in to check out: What other emotions or things am I experiencing today?
_____.

My latest self-takeaway: _____.

Reflection: What do I want to remember from the last question I focused on?

_____

_____

_____

_____

_____

_____

_____

_____

Healing the Narrative

77. Are you aware of the negative thoughts you have upon rising daily? Or throughout the day? Or before you go to sleep? If you answer, "No, I'm not aware of my thoughts," what could you do to become more aware of your negative thoughts? Example: Upon waking for the day, pause momentarily and bring awareness to what you are thinking. Identify what types of thoughts occur and how fast they occur. Are the thoughts negative? Are the thoughts positive? Are the thoughts critical? Do the thoughts feel anxious? Do the thoughts feel sad? Do the thoughts feel confusing? Explore and describe what types of thoughts you are having before the start of your day. Thoughts can influence the type of day you have. If you are aware, you have the power to shift your thoughts. You have to catch them to shift them.

_____

_____

_____

_____

_____

_____

_____

_____

_____

_____

_____

_____

_____

Set the Mood and Tone for Today's Journaling

Date and Time: _____ Location: _____.

Today my sound choice is: _____

Smells, if any: _____ Drinking or eating anything: _____.

I am looking at and noticing _____ surrounding me.

Tasks I accomplished today: _____.

How accomplished I feel today: 1   2   3   4   5

I am taking a break from _____. I give myself permission to get

back up and start _____ again on/at_____.

Check in to check out: What other emotions or things am I experiencing today?
_____.

My latest self-takeaway: _____.

Reflection: What do I want to remember from the last question I focused on?

_____

_____

_____

_____

_____

_____

_____

Healing the Narrative

78. What are you afraid of? I mean, *deathly afraid* of? Dig deep for your answers here.

Example: I am deathly afraid of love. I want it, but I'm afraid of it. Go figure. It took me several journal entries and reflective thought-processing to come back to the tears streaming down my face, telling me my truth and my history: You want love, yet you are *deathly afraid* of it. Now, unpack that.

Set the Mood and Tone for Today's Journaling

Date and Time: _____   Location: _____.

Today my sound choice is: _____.

Smells, if any: _____ Drinking or eating anything: _____.

I am looking at and noticing _____ surrounding me.

Tasks I accomplished today: _____.

How accomplished I feel today: 1   2   3   4   5

I am taking a break from _____. I give myself permission to get

back up and start _____ again on/at _____.

Check in to check out: What other emotions or things am I experiencing today?
_____.

My latest self-takeaway: _____.

Reflection: What do I want to remember from the last question I focused on?

_____

_____

_____

_____

_____

_____

_____

79. What is worrisome? Fear can show up in the body in different ways. Fear can keep you from doing uncertain things and trying uneasy things. Two ways that fear can translate into your mind and body are through <u>F</u>alse <u>E</u>vidence <u>A</u>ppearing <u>R</u>eal, or <u>F</u>orget <u>E</u>verything <u>a</u>nd <u>R</u>un. What do you worry about personally? What do you worry about professionally? Who do you worry about? Who do you think worries about you? Please list people who evoke worry or fear in you. Please make another list of people you worry about. Why, and what is worrisome about the people you named? Unpack any additional worries you hold in your mind. Are the worries real or perceived? What tells you they are real? What tells you they are perceived?

Set the Mood and Tone for Today's Journaling

Date and Time: _____ Location: _____.

Today my sound choice is: _____

Smells, if any: _____ Drinking or eating anything: _____.

I am looking at and noticing _____ surrounding me.

Tasks I accomplished today: _____.

How accomplished I feel today: 1 2 3 4 5

I am taking a break from _____. I give myself permission to get

back up and start _____ again on/at _____.

Check in to check out: What other emotions or things am I experiencing today?
_____.

My latest self-takeaway: _____.

Reflection: What do I want to remember from the last question I focused on?

_____

_____

_____

_____

_____

_____

_____

80. Are you ready to go deep? When we are asked, "Are you ready to go deep?" we often answer on the surface. But if we are bold enough to say yes, we might be surprised by what comes about. Sometimes, it takes time for the answer to reveal itself fully as we allow it to penetrate our souls and draw out our responses little by little. We know that we have arrived at the final answer when we feel satisfied with our response after checking in with our mind, spirit, and body. So be ready for what's to come and give yourself permission to receive the final answer. Make space for more capacity, clarity, and confidence, and don't be afraid to lose control if needed. Share more, say more, and embrace all that comes with going deep. Then re-center.

_____

_____

_____

_____

_____

_____

_____

_____

_____

_____

_____

_____

_____

_____

Set the Mood and Tone for Today's Journaling

Date and Time: _____ Location: _____.

Today my sound choice is: _____

Smells, if any: _____ Drinking or eating anything: _____.

I am looking at and noticing _____ surrounding me.

Tasks I accomplished today: _____.

How accomplished I feel today: 1   2   3   4   5

I am taking a break from _____. I give myself permission to get

back up and start _____ again on/at _____.

Check in to check out: What other emotions or things am I experiencing today?
_____.

My latest self-takeaway: _____.

Reflection: What do I want to remember from the last question I focused on?

_____

_____

_____

_____

_____

_____

_____

Healing the Narrative

81. When you hear the saying, "What happens in this house stays in this house," what comes up for you? What needs to be resolved when you hear this? What needs to be dissolved when you hear this statement? What can you tell yourself about this statement as an evolving human being? Rewrite this statement to give it meaning. How do you allow this statement to hold you still? Or destroy your capability to tell others what is most sacred and trust them with it? What part of this statement can you free yourself from and let go of?

Set the Mood and Tone for Today's Journaling

Date and Time: _____ Location: _____.

Today my sound choice is: _____.

Smells, if any: _____ Drinking or eating anything: _____.

I am looking at and noticing _____ surrounding me.

Tasks I accomplished today: _____.

How accomplished I feel today: 1   2   3   4   5

I am taking a break from _____. I give myself permission to get

back up and start _____ again on/at _____.

Check in to check out: What other emotions or things am I experiencing today?
_____.

My latest self-takeaway: _____.

Reflection: What do I want to remember from the last question I focused on?

_____

_____

_____

_____

_____

_____

_____

Healing the Narrative

82. If you're a trauma survivor: What happened to you?

83. Do you feel unpacked? What else do you need to unpack around this topic? If other things come out, make a separate entry for each item so you know what things you are currently working on, and check them off as you arrive at your level of satisfaction.

_____
_____
_____
_____
_____
_____
_____
_____
_____
_____
_____
_____
_____
_____
_____
_____
_____

Set the Mood and Tone for Today's Journaling

Date and Time: _____ Location: _____.

Today my sound choice is: _____

Smells, if any: _____ Drinking or eating anything: _____.

I am looking at and noticing _____ surrounding me.

Tasks I accomplished today: _____.

How accomplished I feel today: 1   2   3   4   5

I am taking a break from _____. I give myself permission to get

back up and start _____ again on/at _____.

Check in to check out: What other emotions or things am I experiencing today?
_____.

My latest self-takeaway: _____.

Reflection: What do I want to remember from the last question I focused on?

_____

_____

_____

_____

_____

_____

_____

Healing the Narrative

84. If you're a drama survivor: What is happening? Is it serving you and/or your life? If not, why are you still inside or connected to it? This is not a blaming question, but rather a clarification and awareness question. Always know why you are still inside or connected to the drama.

Set the Mood and Tone for Today's Journaling

Date and Time: _____ Location: _____.

Today my sound choice is: _____.

Smells, if any: _____ Drinking or eating anything: _____.

I am looking at and noticing _____ surrounding me.

Tasks I accomplished today: _____.

How accomplished I feel today: 1   2   3   4   5

I am taking a break from _____. I give myself permission to get

back up and start _____ again on/at _____.

Check in to check out: What other emotions or things am I experiencing today?
_____.

My latest self-takeaway: _____.

Reflection: What do I want to remember from the last question I focused on?

_____

_____

_____

_____

_____

_____

_____

85. What are some of your triggers? This question encourages you to think about different categories or types of triggers, such as the following:

   a. Your family
   b. Your friends
   c. Peers or coworkers
   d. Leaders, managers, supervisors, your boss
   e. Intimate partners
   f. Your children or children you care for personally or professionally
   g. Your siblings and/or parents
   h. Others
   i. Other races
   j. People with presumed power over you, or less power than you
   k. Yourself
   l. Specific sounds
   m. Specific textures or things you touch
   n. Specific smells and/or tastes
   o. Specific feelings or emotions
   p. Pressure from stress and overwhelm
   q. Being bored, or having too much free time
   r. Being surprised
   s. Being thought about by others, or not being considered or included
   t. Feeling disappointed or excited
   u. Being loved
   v. Being vulnerable

86. Whose stuff is this anyway? Sort it out in this table.

Your Stuff	Their Stuff
What's your stuff?	What's the other person's stuff?
What can you do to work through your stuff?	What can you do to give the other person's stuff back, and not receive it? It is not yours!

NOTE: *It may require some effort to learn how to differentiate between what belongs to you (stuff) and what belongs to others (stuff), such as family members, elders, significant others, friends, colleagues, and acquaintances. Remember that these things are not yours, and you have a right to decline them.*

87. What emotions come up as you answer these questions? Examine those emotions, and don't run from them. Some will be uncomfortable if pain is attached, yet they can be healed once you are aware of what they are and what they do inside your body.

What else do these emotions bring up? Sometimes emotions have other history and painful memories attached to them, so a floodgate opens when that history or a certain memory comes up. Here come so many other feelings, flashbacks, and other things you were unprepared for. Ask yourself if you can be ready to sit through the pain. Just like other things we encounter for the first time, it might not be easy. But over time, it will become more tolerable. It may always hurt, but facing and sitting with the emotions will help ease the pain until you can finally say, "This is painful, yes, but I am still okay." Don't stuff it down; allow it to be.

88. What's it like when your stuff meets somebody else's stuff? Think and write about what happens when you are confronted with another person's challenges, drama, etc. Is it easy to identify when this happens? What can you do differently when this happens in the future?

Set the Mood and Tone for Today's Journaling

Date and Time: _____   Location: _____.

Today my sound choice is: _____.

Smells, if any: _____ Drinking or eating anything: _____.

I am looking at and noticing _____ surrounding me.

Tasks I accomplished today: _____.

How accomplished I feel today: 1   2   3   4   5

I am taking a break from _____. I give myself permission to get

back up and start _____ again on/at _____.

Check in to check out: What other emotions or things am I experiencing today?
_____.

My latest self-takeaway: _____.

Reflection: What do I want to remember from the last question I focused on?

_____

_____

_____

_____

_____

_____

_____

Healing the Narrative

89. What does freedom look like? What comes to mind when you think about the statement freedom over fear? Are there other things or emotional states you want to consider freeing yourself of? Like, freedom from conformity? Or from anger? Or from feelings of failure? From your past? From things that negatively and positively bound you? From so many things on your to-do list and overall life-work list?

___

90. How will you know you are free of these things? What would you tell me, if we knew each other in real life?

Set the Mood and Tone for Today's Journaling

Date and Time: _____ Location: _____.

Today my sound choice is: _____

Smells, if any: _____ Drinking or eating anything: _____.

I am looking at and noticing _____ surrounding me.

Tasks I accomplished today: _____.

How accomplished I feel today: 1   2   3   4   5

I am taking a break from _____. I give myself permission to get

back up and start _____ again on/at _____.

Check in to check out: What other emotions or things am I experiencing today?
_____.

My latest self-takeaway: _____.

Reflection: What do I want to remember from the last question I focused on?

_____

_____

_____

_____

_____

_____

_____

Healing the Narrative

91. Did you know that trauma can be passed down generationally? What do you think has been passed down to you? What can you identify (or "catch") that you may pass down if you don't bring awareness to it? Refer back to your answers for questions 86 and 87.

Set the Mood and Tone for Today's Journaling

Date and Time: _____ Location: _____.

Today my sound choice is: _____

Smells, if any: _____ Drinking or eating anything: _____.

I am looking at and noticing _____ surrounding me.

Tasks I accomplished today: _____.

How accomplished I feel today: 1   2   3   4   5

I am taking a break from _____. I give myself permission to get back up and start _____ again on/at _____.

Check in to check out: What other emotions or things am I experiencing today?
_____.

My latest self-takeaway: _____.

Reflection: What do I want to remember from the last question I focused on?

_____

_____

_____

_____

_____

_____

_____

92. Do you see your hurt and trauma as your fault? Do you believe your healing experiences are your responsibility? You are responsible for your healing, meaning it is your work now to feel better. Do you think that is an unfair expectation? Discuss here why you answered the way you did. And know that you can call on your village to support you. Remember who you wrote about in your answer to questions 62 and 64. These are the folks you need to help you get through this.

_____
_____
_____
_____
_____
_____
_____
_____
_____
_____
_____
_____
_____
_____

Set the Mood and Tone for Today's Journaling

Date and Time: _____ Location: _____.

Today my sound choice is: _____.

Smells, if any: _____ Drinking or eating anything: _____.

I am looking at and noticing _____ surrounding me.

Tasks I accomplished today: _____.

How accomplished I feel today: 1   2   3   4   5

I am taking a break from _____. I give myself permission to get

back up and start _____ again on/at _____.

Check in to check out: What other emotions or things am I experiencing today?
_____.

My latest self-takeaway: _____.

Reflection: What do I want to remember from the last question I focused on?

_____

_____

_____

_____

_____

_____

_____

_____

Healing the Narrative

93. What do you want to try that you're afraid of doing? Whose voice is in your head, telling you that you can't do it?

Set the Mood and Tone for Today's Journaling

Date and Time: _____   Location: _____.

Today my sound choice is: _____

Smells, if any: _____ Drinking or eating anything: _____.

I am looking at and noticing _____ surrounding me.

Tasks I accomplished today: _____.

How accomplished I feel today: 1   2   3   4   5

I am taking a break from _____. I give myself permission to get back up and start _____ again on/at _____.

Check in to check out: What other emotions or things am I experiencing today?
_____.

My latest self-takeaway: _____.

Reflection: What do I want to remember from the last question I focused on?

_____

_____

_____

_____

_____

_____

_____

Healing the Narrative

94. Let's think about statements or sayings other people have told you that are not serving you. Refer back to your stuff activities in questions 86 and 87.

Here's an example of what I'm talking about. One of the elders in my family used to tell me, "You are lazy if you don't get up and make the bed." Even though this person doesn't say that anymore, I would hear this statement in my head each time I wanted to lie in bed "lazily" on a Saturday. Now, I tell myself that I work hard Monday through Friday, I deserve to rest and fully enjoy my day, and I love my bed messy and my pj's. I have also incorporated my new thoughts and words into my monthly routine. One Saturday a month, I do whatever I want, and I don't even leave the house.

    a. What's one statement or saying you say to yourself most often?

    b. What's one statement or saying you hear constantly that you wish to discard? What can you do to help yourself discard that statement/saying?

    c. Who are you assigning that saying or statement back to? Whose is it? Can you think about how you will assign the saying/statement back to the other person?

    d. Please write about your new habits, practices, or changes you will incorporate as part of your discarding process.

Set the Mood and Tone for Today's Journaling

Date and Time: _____ Location: _____.

Today my sound choice is: _____.

Smells, if any: _____ Drinking or eating anything: _____.

I am looking at and noticing _____ surrounding me.

Tasks I accomplished today: _____.

How accomplished I feel today: 1   2   3   4   5

I am taking a break from _____. I give myself permission to get

back up and start _____ again on/at _____.

Check in to check out: What other emotions or things am I experiencing today?
_____.

My latest self-takeaway: _____.

Reflection: What do I want to remember from the last question I focused on?

_____

_____

_____

_____

_____

_____

_____

95. What are you healing at the moment? What's standing in the way of your healing? What resources do you have to complete the healing process? Will you allow yourself to access the resources you need when you need them? Healing is not easily accessible by any means, but it is possible.

Set the Mood and Tone for Today's Journaling

Date and Time: _____ Location: _____.

Today my sound choice is: _____

Smells, if any: _____ Drinking or eating anything: _____.

I am looking at and noticing _____ surrounding me.

Tasks I accomplished today: _____.

How accomplished I feel today: 1   2   3   4   5

I am taking a break from _____. I give myself permission to get

back up and start _____ again on/at _____.

Check in to check out: What other emotions or things am I experiencing today?
_____.

My latest self-takeaway: _____.

Reflection: What do I want to remember from the last question I focused on?

_____

_____

_____

_____

_____

_____

_____

Healing the Narrative

96. You are the co-author and star of your story. What message do you want to convey about yourself to others? What are your top priorities in life? What are the things that hold no importance to you? What are the things that you can proudly claim as your achievements, knowing that you are your own hero and storyteller? What are the areas where you feel that others have misunderstood you the most? What is your superpower?

_____
_____
_____
_____
_____
_____
_____
_____
_____
_____
_____
_____
_____
_____
_____
_____
_____

Set the Mood and Tone for Today's Journaling

Date and Time: _____ Location: _____.

Today my sound choice is: _____

Smells, if any: _____ Drinking or eating anything: _____.

I am looking at and noticing _____ surrounding me.

Tasks I accomplished today: _____.

How accomplished I feel today: 1   2   3   4   5

I am taking a break from _____. I give myself permission to get

back up and start _____ again on/at _____.

Check in to check out: What other emotions or things am I experiencing today?
_____.

My latest self-takeaway: _____.

Reflection: What do I want to remember from the last question I focused on?

_____

_____

_____

_____

_____

_____

_____

Healing the Narrative

97. Reflect on this idea and share your thoughts below: Self-work increases self-worth! Do you agree with that statement? Explain why or why not. Talk about what it will look like for you to take the time to work on yourself and maintain your worth at all costs. You are so worth it. Do you think and feel like you are worth something? Value to yourself? Value to others? Elaborate more here.

_____

_____

_____

_____

_____

_____

_____

_____

_____

_____

_____

_____

_____

_____

_____

_____

_____

Set the Mood and Tone for Today's Journaling

Date and Time: _____ Location: _____.

Today my sound choice is: _____

Smells, if any: _____ Drinking or eating anything: _____.

I am looking at and noticing _____ surrounding me.

Tasks I accomplished today: _____.

How accomplished I feel today: 1   2   3   4   5

I am taking a break from _____. I give myself permission to get back up and start _____ again on/at _____.

Check in to check out: What other emotions or things am I experiencing today?
_____.

My latest self-takeaway: _____.

Reflection: What do I want to remember from the last question I focused on?

_____

_____

_____

_____

_____

_____

_____

98. What does your mess look like? How does your mess show up in your life? Is it your mess, or are you mixed into the mess of others? You must name your mess to understand your message. Think about that. Now what is your message? Your message to yourself? Your message to others? How do you show up in the world? How do you think others see you in the world? Your mess is your message. I once heard someone say, "YOU ARE BOTH A MESS AND A MASTERPIECE AT THE SAME DAMN TIME!" How do you resonate with that statement?

_____
_____
_____
_____
_____
_____
_____
_____
_____
_____
_____
_____
_____
_____

99. What does your masterpiece look like? In other words, what does it look like when you are operating as your best self? Reflect on the similarities and differences between this and what you wrote in question 51.

Set the Mood and Tone for Today's Journaling

Date and Time: _____ Location: _____.

Today my sound choice is: _____

Smells, if any: _____ Drinking or eating anything: _____.

I am looking at and noticing _____ surrounding me.

Tasks I accomplished today: _____.

How accomplished I feel today: 1 2 3 4 5

I am taking a break from _____. I give myself permission to get

back up and start _____ again on/at _____.

Check in to check out: What other emotions or things am I experiencing today?
_____.

My latest self-takeaway: _____.

Reflection: What do I want to remember from the last question I focused on?

_____

_____

_____

_____

_____

_____

_____

_____

Healing the Narrative

100. Describe yourself. How do you show up in the world? Who are you in the skin you are in? How comfortable are you in your own body? How old are you? What do you look like? What does your skin feel like? Who are you? In friendships? In the workplace? In conversation with a same-sex person? With a person of the opposite sex? In your community? In group settings? When you are by yourself? In your culture? In different cultures? In spaces where you are othered?

_____

_____

_____

_____

_____

_____

_____

_____

_____

_____

_____

_____

_____

_____

_____

_____

Pause Moment #6

Nothing will feel perfect.

It just has to be good enough.

Nothing ever truly feels perfect. But sometimes, good enough is all we need.

Take a deep breath in and ask yourself, "What am I breathing in?" Exhale slowly and ask yourself, "What am I breathing out?" Repeat this process several times, taking intentional, healthy breaths of air. Let out a huge and loud sigh, making the "ahhhh" sound. Allow yourself to slow down and breathe with peace. Remember that you deserve regular, restorative breaths of fresh air. Take soft, unhurried breaths that feel normal and joyful. Your body deserves this moment of calm and relaxation.

level up and thrive

Set the Mood and Tone for Today's Journaling

Date and Time: _____ Location: _____.

Today my sound choice is: _____.

Smells, if any: _____ Drinking or eating anything: _____.

I am looking at and noticing _____ surrounding me.

Tasks I accomplished today: _____.

How accomplished I feel today: 1   2   3   4   5

I am taking a break from _____. I give myself permission to get

back up and start _____ again on/at _____.

Check in to check out: What other emotions or things am I experiencing today?
_____.

My latest self-takeaway: _____.

Reflection: What do I want to remember from the last question I focused on?

_____

_____

_____

_____

_____

_____

_____

101. What's your next-level desire? What is the highest level you want to achieve? How will you know you are there? Will you pivot if the journey calls you to do so?

_____
_____
_____
_____
_____
_____
_____
_____
_____
_____
_____
_____
_____
_____
_____
_____
_____
_____
_____
_____
_____
_____

Set the Mood and Tone for Today's Journaling

Date and Time: _____ Location: _____.

Today my sound choice is: _____

Smells, if any: _____ Drinking or eating anything: _____.

I am looking at and noticing _____ surrounding me.

Tasks I accomplished today: _____.

How accomplished I feel today: 1   2   3   4   5

I am taking a break from _____. I give myself permission to get

back up and start _____ again on/at _____.

Check in to check out: What other emotions or things am I experiencing today?
_____.

My latest self-takeaway: _____.

Reflection: What do I want to remember from the last question I focused on?

_____

_____

_____

_____

_____

_____

_____

102. Do you feel you have strong self-worth? Or strong self-esteem? See your responses for question 97.

  a. Do you know the difference between self-worth and self-esteem? If so, how are they different?

  b. Do you ever discount yourself or your worth? If so, why? If not, what keeps you from discounting your worth? Or from allowing others to have access to you when they are not worthy?

Level Up and Thrive

Set the Mood and Tone for Today's Journaling

Date and Time: _____   Location: _____.

Today my sound choice is: _____

Smells, if any: _____ Drinking or eating anything: _____.

I am looking at and noticing _____ surrounding me.

Tasks I accomplished today: _____.

How accomplished I feel today: 1   2   3   4   5

I am taking a break from _____. I give myself permission to get

back up and start _____ again on/at _____.

Check in to check out: What other emotions or things am I experiencing today?
_____.

My latest self-takeaway: _____.

Reflection: What do I want to remember from the last question I focused on?

_____

_____

_____

_____

_____

_____

_____

Level Up and Thrive

103. How have the different pieces of your life come together for the greater good? List the parts of your life you want to bring back together to feel whole. Think about the different working and moving parts of your life as you imagine its fullness. As you move through various questions in this journal, what different angles can you think of for this question?

Set the Mood and Tone for Today's Journaling

Date and Time: _____ Location: _____.

Today my sound choice is: _____

Smells, if any: _____ Drinking or eating anything: _____.

I am looking at and noticing _____ surrounding me.

Tasks I accomplished today: _____

How accomplished I feel today: 1   2   3   4   5

I am taking a break from _____. I give myself permission to get

back up and start _____ again on/at _____.

Check in to check out: What other emotions or things am I experiencing today?
_____.

My latest self-takeaway: _____.

Reflection: What do I want to remember from the last question I focused on?

_____

_____

_____

_____

_____

_____

_____

_____

Level Up and Thrive

104. Do you see your self-work reflected in your family? What about your daily activities? Your choices? Your relationships? Your faith walk? Your conversations with others? Your adventures? Or your lack thereof? Your workflow? Your material goals? Your mindset? Are you satisfied thus far? If not, what do you need to be satisfied? Or see the results you want?

_____
_____
_____
_____
_____
_____
_____
_____
_____
_____
_____
_____
_____
_____
_____

Set the Mood and Tone for Today's Journaling

Date and Time: _____　　Location: _____.

Today my sound choice is: _____

Smells, if any: _____ Drinking or eating anything: _____.

I am looking at and noticing _____ surrounding me.

Tasks I accomplished today: _____.

How accomplished I feel today:　　1　　2　　3　　4　　5

I am taking a break from _____. I give myself permission to get

back up and start _____ again on/at _____.

Check in to check out: What other emotions or things am I experiencing today?
_____.

My latest self-takeaway: _____.

Reflection: What do I want to remember from the last question I focused on?

_____

_____

_____

_____

_____

_____

_____

105. Who do you consult with when you are going through a challenge? Think, then write, about why you turn to these individuals. When you consult with these individuals, are you satisfied with the help you receive?

Set the Mood and Tone for Today's Journaling

Date and Time: _____   Location: _____.

Today my sound choice is: _____.

Smells, if any: _____ Drinking or eating anything: _____.

I am looking at and noticing _____ surrounding me.

Tasks I accomplished today: _____.

How accomplished I feel today: 1   2   3   4   5

I am taking a break from _____. I give myself permission to get

back up and start _____ again on/at _____.

Check in to check out: What other emotions or things am I experiencing today?
_____.

My latest self-takeaway: _____.

Reflection: What do I want to remember from the last question I focused on?

_____

_____

_____

_____

_____

_____

_____

Level Up and Thrive

106. How do you receive clarity? What does clarity look or feel like to you? If you are unsure how to receive clarity, what could you do to make yourself more open to receiving it regularly?

Set the Mood and Tone for Today's Journaling

Date and Time: _____   Location: _____.

Today my sound choice is: _____.

Smells, if any: _____ Drinking or eating anything: _____.

I am looking at and noticing _____ surrounding me.

Tasks I accomplished today: _____.

How accomplished I feel today: 1   2   3   4   5

I am taking a break from _____. I give myself permission to get

back up and start _____ again on/at _____.

Check in to check out: What other emotions or things am I experiencing today?
_____.

My latest self-takeaway: _____.

Reflection: What do I want to remember from the last question I focused on?

_____

_____

_____

_____

_____

_____

_____

107. How do you know you are competent at something? How do you know you feel confident? Or if you're lacking confidence?

Set the Mood and Tone for Today's Journaling

Date and Time: _____ Location: _____.

Today my sound choice is: _____

Smells, if any: _____ Drinking or eating anything: _____.

I am looking at and noticing _____ surrounding me.

Tasks I accomplished today: _____.

How accomplished I feel today: 1   2   3   4   5

I am taking a break from _____. I give myself permission to get

back up and start _____ again on/at _____.

Check in to check out: What other emotions or things am I experiencing today?
_____.

My latest self-takeaway: _____.

Reflection: What do I want to remember from the last question I focused on?

_____

_____

_____

_____

_____

_____

_____

108. What's your way to ensure balance? What would that look like or feel like for you?

Set the Mood and Tone for Today's Journaling

Date and Time: _____ Location: _____.

Today my sound choice is: _____.

Smells, if any: _____ Drinking or eating anything: _____.

I am looking at and noticing _____ surrounding me.

Tasks I accomplished today: _____.

How accomplished I feel today: 1   2   3   4   5

I am taking a break from _____. I give myself permission to get

back up and start _____ again on/at _____.

Check in to check out: What other emotions or things am I experiencing today?
_____.

My latest self-takeaway: _____.

Reflection: What do I want to remember from the last question I focused on?

_____

_____

_____

_____

_____

_____

_____

109. What's your fantasy for your professional life? Can you write about this fantasy in as much detail as possible? Go all out in your fantasy. Remember to dream big.

Set the Mood and Tone for Today's Journaling

Date and Time: _____ Location: _____.

Today my sound choice is: _____

Smells, if any: _____ Drinking or eating anything: _____.

I am looking at and noticing _____ surrounding me.

Tasks I accomplished today: _____.

How accomplished I feel today: 1   2   3   4   5

I am taking a break from _____. I give myself permission to get

back up and start _____ again on/at_____.

Check in to check out: What other emotions or things am I experiencing today?
_____.

My latest self-takeaway: _____.

Reflection: What do I want to remember from the last question I focused on?

_____

_____

_____

_____

_____

_____

_____

Level Up and Thrive

110. What do you need to allow yourself to heal from?

Set the Mood and Tone for Today's Journaling

Date and Time: _____ Location: _____.

Today my sound choice is: _____.

Smells, if any: _____ Drinking or eating anything: _____.

I am looking at and noticing _____ surrounding me.

Tasks I accomplished today: _____.

How accomplished I feel today: 1   2   3   4   5

I am taking a break from _____. I give myself permission to get

back up and start _____ again on/at _____.

Check in to check out: What other emotions or things am I experiencing today?
_____.

My latest self-takeaway: _____.

Reflection: What do I want to remember from the last question I focused on?

_____

_____

_____

_____

_____

_____

_____

Level Up and Thrive

111. What do you need to forgive yourself? Or to forgive other people? Has anyone ever hurt you so badly that you made a decision to never forgive them? If so, what was the thing they did so badly to hurt you?

Set the Mood and Tone for Today's Journaling

Date and Time: _____ Location: _____.

Today my sound choice is: _____

Smells, if any: _____ Drinking or eating anything: _____.

I am looking at and noticing _____ surrounding me.

Tasks I accomplished today: _____

How accomplished I feel today: 1   2   3   4   5

I am taking a break from _____. I give myself permission to get

back up and start _____ again on/at _____.

Check in to check out: What other emotions or things am I experiencing today?
_____.

My latest self-takeaway: _____.

Reflection: What do I want to remember from the last question I focused on?

_____

_____

_____

_____

_____

_____

_____

Level Up and Thrive

112. Are you enjoying the fruits of your labor? If so, how? If not, what can you change so you can begin to enjoy them?

Set the Mood and Tone for Today's Journaling

Date and Time: _____ Location: _____.

Today my sound choice is: _____

Smells, if any: _____ Drinking or eating anything: _____.

I am looking at and noticing _____ surrounding me.

Tasks I accomplished today: _____

How accomplished I feel today: 1   2   3   4   5

I am taking a break from _____. I give myself permission to get

back up and start _____ again on/at _____.

Check in to check out: What other emotions or things am I experiencing today?
_____.

My latest self-takeaway: _____.

Reflection: What do I want to remember from the last question I focused on?

_____

_____

_____

_____

_____

_____

_____

Level Up and Thrive

113. What shifts in mindset do you desire? What shifts have you made recently? What shifts will you make moving forward? How will you measure whether you have achieved that shift?

Set the Mood and Tone for Today's Journaling

Date and Time: _____ Location: _____.

Today my sound choice is: _____.

Smells, if any: _____ Drinking or eating anything: _____.

I am looking at and noticing _____ surrounding me.

Tasks I accomplished today: _____.

How accomplished I feel today:　　1　　2　　3　　4　　5

I am taking a break from _____. I give myself permission to get

back up and start _____ again on/at _____.

Check in to check out: What other emotions or things am I experiencing today?
_____.

My latest self-takeaway: _____.

Reflection: What do I want to remember from the last question I focused on?

_____

_____

_____

_____

_____

_____

_____

_____

114. Explain how you get up daily and get yourself together even when you don't feel like it.
Take your time here. The struggle is real!

Set the Mood and Tone for Today's Journaling

Date and Time: _____ Location: _____.

Today my sound choice is: _____

Smells, if any: _____ Drinking or eating anything: _____.

I am looking at and noticing _____ surrounding me.

Tasks I accomplished today: _____.

How accomplished I feel today: 1   2   3   4   5

I am taking a break from _____. I give myself permission to get

back up and start _____ again on/at _____.

Check in to check out: What other emotions or things am I experiencing today?
_____.

My latest self-takeaway: _____.

Reflection: What do I want to remember from the last question I focused on?

_____

_____

_____

_____

_____

_____

_____

115. What do you need to give yourself permission to do? What do you need to allow yourself NOT to do? What do you need to allow yourself to accept? To reject? To be happy with? To move on from?

Set the Mood and Tone for Today's Journaling

Date and Time: _____   Location: _____.

Today my sound choice is: _____

Smells, if any: _____ Drinking or eating anything: _____.

I am looking at and noticing _____ surrounding me.

Tasks I accomplished today: _____.

How accomplished I feel today: 1   2   3   4   5

I am taking a break from _____. I give myself permission to get

back up and start _____ again on/at _____.

Check in to check out: What other emotions or things am I experiencing today?
_____.

My latest self-takeaway: _____.

Reflection: What do I want to remember from the last question I focused on?

_____

_____

_____

_____

_____

_____

_____

Level Up and Thrive

116. What mistakes are you making repeatedly? What can you learn from them? Do you think you are still learning something from the mistake if you continue to make it?

Set the Mood and Tone for Today's Journaling

Date and Time: _____ Location: _____.

Today my sound choice is: _____

Smells, if any: _____ Drinking or eating anything: _____.

I am looking at and noticing _____ surrounding me.

Tasks I accomplished today: _____.

How accomplished I feel today: 1   2   3   4   5

I am taking a break from _____. I give myself permission to get

back up and start _____ again on/at _____.

Check in to check out: What other emotions or things am I experiencing today?
_____.

My latest self-takeaway: _____.

Reflection: What do I want to remember from the last question I focused on?

_____

_____

_____

_____

_____

_____

_____

Level Up and Thrive

117. What will happen if you do not get out of your own way? And, what will happen if you do?

Set the Mood and Tone for Today's Journaling

Date and Time: _____ Location: _____.

Today my sound choice is: _____

Smells, if any: _____ Drinking or eating anything: _____.

I am looking at and noticing _____ surrounding me.

Tasks I accomplished today: _____.

How accomplished I feel today: 1   2   3   4   5

I am taking a break from _____. I give myself permission to get back up and start _____ again on/at _____.

Check in to check out: What other emotions or things am I experiencing today?
_____.

My latest self-takeaway: _____.

Reflection: What do I want to remember from the last question I focused on?

_____

_____

_____

_____

_____

_____

_____

Level Up and Thrive

118. Did you know that you are not your trauma? Can you further explore and explain your answer beyond a simple yes or no response? For instance, if you answer, "No, I didn't know that I am not my trauma," why do you believe this? Did you ever hear the word trauma while you were growing up? Is trauma a helpful word to you? To your community? Why and why not?

Can you define your understanding of trauma? Personal trauma? Workplace trauma? Childhood trauma?

_____

_____

_____

_____

_____

_____

_____

_____

_____

_____

_____

_____

_____

_____

Set the Mood and Tone for Today's Journaling

Date and Time: _____   Location: _____.

Today my sound choice is: _____

Smells, if any: _____   Drinking or eating anything: _____.

I am looking at and noticing _____ surrounding me.

Tasks I accomplished today: _____.

How accomplished I feel today: 1   2   3   4   5

I am taking a break from _____. I give myself permission to get

back up and start _____ again on/at _____.

Check in to check out: What other emotions or things am I experiencing today?
_____.

My latest self-takeaway: _____.

Reflection: What do I want to remember from the last question I focused on?

_____

_____

_____

_____

_____

_____

_____

Level Up and Thrive

119. Did you know that you are responsible for your journey through healing? Can you explore your answer beyond a simple yes or no response? For instance, if your answer is, "No, I didn't know that I was responsible for my healing journey," talk about why you believe this. Where and from whom does this belief come from?

___
___
___
___
___
___
___
___
___
___
___
___
___
___
___
___
___
___

Set the Mood and Tone for Today's Journaling

Date and Time: _____ Location: _____.

Today my sound choice is: _____

Smells, if any: _____ Drinking or eating anything: _____.

I am looking at and noticing _____ surrounding me.

Tasks I accomplished today: _____.

How accomplished I feel today: 1   2   3   4   5

I am taking a break from _____. I give myself permission to get back up and start _____ again on/at _____.

Check in to check out: What other emotions or things am I experiencing today?
_____.

My latest self-takeaway: _____.

Reflection: What do I want to remember from the last question I focused on?

_____
_____
_____
_____
_____
_____
_____

Level Up and Thrive

120. Did you know that you can change the patterns or pathways for the next generation? This is also true in your intimate and/or social relationships with others. We project what we don't want onto others and are sometimes unaware that traumatic experiences exist in our relationships. This can lead us to think about how messed up we are or how others have messed us up, because we repeat cycles we are often unaware of or feel helpless to do anything about. Protect the next generation from traumatic experiences, one piece of trauma or drama at a time.

_____
_____
_____
_____
_____
_____
_____
_____
_____
_____
_____
_____
_____
_____
_____

Set the Mood and Tone for Today's Journaling

Date and Time: _____   Location: _____.

Today my sound choice is: _____.

Smells, if any: _____ Drinking or eating anything: _____.

I am looking at and noticing _____ surrounding me.

Tasks I accomplished today: _____.

How accomplished I feel today: 1   2   3   4   5

I am taking a break from _____. I give myself permission to get

back up and start _____ again on/at _____.

Check in to check out: What other emotions or things am I experiencing today?
_____.

My latest self-takeaway: _____.

Reflection: What do I want to remember from the last question I focused on?

_____

_____

_____

_____

_____

_____

_____

_____

121. Are you ever too hard on yourself? Or, are you too relaxed about things that you need to be sterner with yourself about? If you answer, "Yes, I'm too hard on myself," can you explain why you're so hard on yourself? Can you journal about a recent instance when you were hard on yourself? If you answer, "Yes, I am too relaxed about things that I need to be sterner with myself about," explain where this comes from. What types of things push you to be better?

_____

_____

_____

_____

_____

_____

_____

_____

_____

_____

_____

_____

_____

_____

_____

122. In what ways and areas of your life are you cutting yourself slack? Where are you not cutting yourself slack? What are some reasons why you would not cut yourself some slack? What do you need to not be hard on yourself? What could be helpful?

Set the Mood and Tone for Today's Journaling

Date and Time: _____ Location: _____.

Today my sound choice is: _____.

Smells, if any: _____ Drinking or eating anything: _____.

I am looking at and noticing _____ surrounding me.

Tasks I accomplished today: _____.

How accomplished I feel today: 1   2   3   4   5

I am taking a break from _____. I give myself permission to get

back up and start _____ again on/at _____.

Check in to check out: What other emotions or things am I experiencing today?
_____.

My latest self-takeaway: _____.

Reflection: What do I want to remember from the last question I focused on?

_____

_____

_____

_____

_____

_____

_____

123. What fruits of the spirit do you hold? And, what fruits do you lack? Think about things like joy, faith, belief, trust, peace, and love here.

Set the Mood and Tone for Today's Journaling

Date and Time: _____ Location: _____.

Today my sound choice is: _____.

Smells, if any: _____ Drinking or eating anything: _____.

I am looking at and noticing _____ surrounding me.

Tasks I accomplished today: _____.

How accomplished I feel today: 1   2   3   4   5

I am taking a break from _____. I give myself permission to get

back up and start _____ again on/at _____.

Check in to check out: What other emotions or things am I experiencing today?
_____.

My latest self-takeaway: _____.

Reflection: What do I want to remember from the last question I focused on?

_____

_____

_____

_____

_____

_____

_____

_____

124. What's your exit plan from the following areas of your life? Have you ever thought about what this exit plan would look like?

   a. Work

   b. An unbalanced or stressful home life; your home is no longer suitable

   c. Financial patterns, responsibilities, and obligations that no longer serve you

   d. A challenging situation

   e. Toxic or negative friendships/relationships

   f. Negative family encounters

Set the Mood and Tone for Today's Journaling

Date and Time: _____ Location: _____.

Today my sound choice is: _____

Smells, if any: _____ Drinking or eating anything: _____.

I am looking at and noticing _____ surrounding me.

Tasks I accomplished today: _____.

How accomplished I feel today: 1   2   3   4   5

I am taking a break from _____. I give myself permission to get

back up and start _____ again on/at _____.

Check in to check out: What other emotions or things am I experiencing today?
_____.

My latest self-takeaway: _____.

Reflection: What do I want to remember from the last question I focused on?

_____

_____

_____

_____

_____

_____

_____

Level Up and Thrive

125. How do you engage in self-care? In other words, how do you care for yourself? Moment-to-moment self-care matters! This can look like sips of water; short, gentle movements; giving yourself grace and space; pausing before responding; forgiveness for making mistakes; forgiveness for falling for it again; or forgiveness and healing for not knowing—or for never knowing because you are still growing.

This question was asked before to help you get started, and now it's being asked again to check in with where you are in your self-care journey. Take a moment to reflect on what has worked for you, what hasn't, and what adjustments you may need to make moving forward. Remember, self-care is important, and you should never hesitate to prioritize your own well-being. By making self-care a priority, you can create a healthy and balanced lifestyle that allows you to thrive.

Pause Moment #7

Take your time with your journey.

It's important to take your time on your journey toward healing. Rushing to complete it could lead to boredom.

Take control of your breathing if you can't control anything else. It's interesting to note that the first and last thing every human being "takes" is a breath, from the start of life to its end. Therefore, make the most of every breath you take.

Recall and recap

Set the Mood and Tone for Today's Journaling

Date and Time: _____   Location: _____.

Today my sound choice is: _____.

Smells, if any: _____   Drinking or eating anything: _____.

I am looking at and noticing _____ surrounding me.

Tasks I accomplished today: _____.

How accomplished I feel today: 1   2   3   4   5

I am taking a break from _____. I give myself permission to get

back up and start _____ again on/at _____.

Check in to check out: What other emotions or things am I experiencing today?
_____.

My latest self-takeaway: _____.

Reflection: What do I want to remember from the last question I focused on?

_____

_____

_____

_____

_____

_____

_____

126. Do you feel you have a good chance of being great in this world? Do you know that you are already plentiful and wonderfully made, despite your real or perceived flaws?

Set the Mood and Tone for Today's Journaling

Date and Time: _____ Location: _____.

Today my sound choice is: _____.

Smells, if any: _____ Drinking or eating anything: _____.

I am looking at and noticing _____ surrounding me.

Tasks I accomplished today: _____.

How accomplished I feel today: 1   2   3   4   5

I am taking a break from _____. I give myself permission to get

back up and start _____ again on/at _____.

Check in to check out: What other emotions or things am I experiencing today?
_____.

My latest self-takeaway: _____.

Reflection: What do I want to remember from the last question I focused on?

_____

_____

_____

_____

_____

_____

Recall and Recap

Recall and Recap

127. Have you ever thought about your life stages or situations like levels in a video game? If you answer, "No, I've never thought about life that way before," can you imagine your current situation as a level in a video game? If you answer, "Yes, I've thought about life that way before," can you describe the stages and levels you have had to confront? How do you know you have arrived at the next level? Mastered a stage? At each level, you must confront different challenges and grab all the leverage you can to keep going without being thrown off your path. Remember, there's a different devil for a different level. Be ready for your challenges, and be ready to fight until you make it to the level you want to get to. If this were easy, everyone would be at the same level.

_____

_____

_____

_____

_____

_____

_____

_____

_____

_____

_____

_____

_____

_____

128. What are the progress markers that help you measure your movement? How do they help you evaluate your progress or growth? How do you know when you are moving forward? How do you know when you are regressing or moving backward? How do you know and accept that you are moving reasonably and steadily? When we were babies, we were wired to do smart things by returning to an earlier state of being, which is called regression. We regress at times to fully progress in the right direction. This smart thing continues to help us move forward by going backward to a place of confidence and competence.

Recall and Recap

Set the Mood and Tone for Today's Journaling

Date and Time: _____ Location: _____.

Today my sound choice is: _____.

Smells, if any: _____ Drinking or eating anything: _____.

I am looking at and noticing _____ surrounding me.

Tasks I accomplished today: _____.

How accomplished I feel today: 1   2   3   4   5

I am taking a break from _____. I give myself permission to get

back up and start _____ again on/at_____.

Check in to check out: What other emotions or things am I experiencing today?
_____.

My latest self-takeaway: _____.

Reflection: What do I want to remember from the last question I focused on?

_____

_____

_____

_____

_____

_____

_____

Recall and Recap

129. What do you need to move forward in your journey through healing? What do you need in order to pause? Do you know your cues to pause and take a break? Could you give an example of a task you realize you need a break from and discuss how you will permit yourself to pause?

Set the Mood and Tone for Today's Journaling

Date and Time: _____ Location: _____.

Today my sound choice is: _____

Smells, if any: _____ Drinking or eating anything: _____.

I am looking at and noticing _____ surrounding me.

Tasks I accomplished today: _____.

How accomplished I feel today: 1   2   3   4   5

I am taking a break from _____. I give myself permission to get

back up and start _____ again on/at _____.

Check in to check out: What other emotions or things am I experiencing today?
_____.

My latest self-takeaway: _____.

Reflection: What do I want to remember from the last question I focused on?

_____

_____

_____

_____

_____

_____

Recall and Recap

130. Do you believe healing is possible? What do you know and believe about healing? Does healing happen for a person like you? What do healing possibilities look like specifically for you?

Set the Mood and Tone for Today's Journaling

Date and Time: _____   Location: _____.

Today my sound choice is: _____

Smells, if any: _____ Drinking or eating anything: _____.

I am looking at and noticing _____ surrounding me.

Tasks I accomplished today: _____.

How accomplished I feel today: 1   2   3   4   5

I am taking a break from _____. I give myself permission to get

back up and start _____ again on/at _____.

Check in to check out: What other emotions or things am I experiencing today?
_____.

My latest self-takeaway: _____.

Reflection: What do I want to remember from the last question I focused on?

_____

_____

_____

_____

_____

_____

_____

Recall and Recap

Recall and Recap

131. Read this statement: "I understand that healing is a process." Does this resonate with you? If so, how? How have you come to realize that your healing is a process? How do you plan to continue the healing process outside of this journal? Describe your plan of action to continue your healing journey. Incremental steps are all it takes to move forward and gain traction on your journey. As stated at the beginning of this healing journey, the work that you have embarked on is not easy. One step does not complete the entire process. Each step moves the process closer to your determination of satisfaction. Arriving at the place you have been dreaming of arriving at. Give yourself some credit for making it this far.

_____
_____
_____
_____
_____
_____
_____
_____
_____
_____
_____
_____
_____
_____

Set the Mood and Tone for Today's Journaling

Date and Time: _____ Location: _____.

Today my sound choice is: _____.

Smells, if any: _____ Drinking or eating anything: _____.

I am looking at and noticing _____ surrounding me.

Tasks I accomplished today: _____.

How accomplished I feel today: 1   2   3   4   5

I am taking a break from _____. I give myself permission to get

back up and start _____ again on/at _____.

Check in to check out: What other emotions or things am I experiencing today?
_____.

My latest self-takeaway: _____.

Reflection: What do I want to remember from the last question I focused on?

_____

_____

_____

_____

_____

_____

Recall and Recap

132. Describe your authentic self: In what ways can you show up as your authentic self in life? In friendships? In the workplace? In conversations about race and culture? In your community? In the dominant culture or non-dominant culture? In spaces where you are othered?

Set the Mood and Tone for Today's Journaling

Date and Time: _____ Location: _____.

Today my sound choice is: _____

Smells, if any: _____ Drinking or eating anything: _____.

I am looking at and noticing _____ surrounding me.

Tasks I accomplished today: _____.

How accomplished I feel today: 1   2   3   4   5

I am taking a break from _____. I give myself permission to get

back up and start _____ again on/at _____.

Check in to check out: What other emotions or things am I experiencing today?
_____.

My latest self-takeaway: _____.

Reflection: What do I want to remember from the last question I focused on?

_____

_____

_____

_____

_____

_____

_____

Recall and Recap

133. Who do you want to be? Are you happy being you? Have you ever wanted a different identity or name? If so, what are they? If not, discuss why not. In other words, discuss in what ways you are satisfied being you.

Set the Mood and Tone for Today's Journaling

Date and Time: _____ Location: _____.

Today my sound choice is: _____

Smells, if any: _____ Drinking or eating anything: _____.

I am looking at and noticing _____ surrounding me.

Tasks I accomplished today: _____.

How accomplished I feel today: 1   2   3   4   5

I am taking a break from _____. I give myself permission to get

back up and start _____ again on/at _____.

Check in to check out: What other emotions or things am I experiencing today?
_____.

My latest self-takeaway: _____.

Reflection: What do I want to remember from the last question I focused on?

_____

_____

_____

_____

_____

_____

_____

Recall and Recap

134. How do you show up in the world? How are you present in the things you do? Or with the people you spend time and space with? How are you not present?

Set the Mood and Tone for Today's Journaling

Date and Time: _____ Location: _____.

Today my sound choice is: _____

Smells, if any: _____ Drinking or eating anything: _____.

I am looking at and noticing _____ surrounding me.

Tasks I accomplished today: _____.

How accomplished I feel today: 1   2   3   4   5

I am taking a break from _____. I give myself permission to get

back up and start _____ again on/at _____.

Check in to check out: What other emotions or things am I experiencing today?
_____.

My latest self-takeaway: _____.

Reflection: What do I want to remember from the last question I focused on?

_____

_____

_____

_____

_____

_____

_____

Recall and Recap

135. What is starting to make sense to you on your healing journey? What are some of the discoveries that you have made? What are you spending the most time on? What does not make sense? Is there anything that has surprised you? This is called the meaning-making stage. What can you begin to piece together so that each thing has the proper meaning attached to it?

_____
_____
_____
_____
_____
_____
_____
_____
_____
_____
_____
_____
_____
_____
_____
_____

Set the Mood and Tone for Today's Journaling

Date and Time: _____ Location: _____.

Today my sound choice is: _____.

Smells, if any: _____ Drinking or eating anything: _____.

I am looking at and noticing _____ surrounding me.

Tasks I accomplished today: _____.

How accomplished I feel today: 1   2   3   4   5

I am taking a break from _____. I give myself permission to get

back up and start _____ again on/at _____.

Check in to check out: What other emotions or things am I experiencing today?
_____.

My latest self-takeaway: _____.

Reflection: What do I want to remember from the last question I focused on?

_____

_____

_____

_____

_____

_____

_____

136. What prompts do you need for forward movement? Why do you think certain prompts will help you move forward? What is helpful about having prompts? Have you ever had a thought partner—someone to think things through with? Have you found that this type of partnered thinking is helpful? If you find thought partnering beneficial, is this an area that would prompt you to ask for help as needed?

_____
_____
_____
_____
_____
_____
_____
_____
_____
_____
_____
_____
_____
_____
_____
_____
_____
_____

Set the Mood and Tone for Today's Journaling

Date and Time: _____ Location: _____.

Today my sound choice is: _____.

Smells, if any: _____ Drinking or eating anything: _____.

I am looking at and noticing _____ surrounding me.

Tasks I accomplished today: _____.

How accomplished I feel today: 1   2   3   4   5

I am taking a break from _____. I give myself permission to get

back up and start _____ again on/at _____.

Check in to check out: What other emotions or things am I experiencing today?
_____.

My latest self-takeaway: _____.

Reflection: What do I want to remember from the last question I focused on?

_____

_____

_____

_____

_____

_____

Recall and Recap

137. Where are you now? Any shifts? And where do you want to be?

   a. Are you in the "same place" as when you started this journey? Or are you in a different place now? How does it feel? Where will you go from here?

   b. How will you use the data collected in your journal to move forward?

   c. What do you need to be satisfied with where you are?

   d. Will you allow yourself to not know what may happen next? Or to not always know what may happen? This means trusting yourself and trusting the process. Are you willing to do that? Are you willing to put the pen or computer down and give yourself permission to return to your healing body of work as needed?

Recall and Recap

Recall and Recap

Set the Mood and Tone for Today's Journaling

Date and Time: _____ Location: _____.

Today my sound choice is: _____

Smells, if any: _____ Drinking or eating anything: _____.

I am looking at and noticing _____ surrounding me.

Tasks I accomplished today: _____.

How accomplished I feel today: 1   2   3   4   5

I am taking a break from _____. I give myself permission to get

back up and start _____ again on/at _____.

Check in to check out: What other emotions or things am I experiencing today?
_____.

My latest self-takeaway: _____.

Reflection: What do I want to remember from the last question I focused on?

_____

_____

_____

_____

_____

_____

_____

138. What has been your experience with the work you've done so far? How do you feel at this point in your healing journey? What challenges have come up for you while answering these questions?

_____
_____
_____
_____
_____
_____
_____
_____
_____
_____
_____
_____
_____
_____
_____
_____
_____
_____
_____
_____

Set the Mood and Tone for Today's Journaling

Date and Time: _____   Location: _____.

Today my sound choice is: _____.

Smells, if any: _____   Drinking or eating anything: _____.

I am looking at and noticing _____ surrounding me.

Tasks I accomplished today: _____

How accomplished I feel today: 1   2   3   4   5

I am taking a break from _____. I give myself permission to get back up and start _____ again on/at _____.

Check in to check out: What other emotions or things am I experiencing today?
_____

My latest self-takeaway: _____.

Reflection: What do I want to remember from the last question I focused on?

_____

_____

_____

_____

_____

_____

Recall and Recap

139. Read this statement: "It is not easy telling others just how messed up I am." Does this resonate with you? If so, how?

Set the Mood and Tone for Today's Journaling

Date and Time: _____   Location: _____.

Today my sound choice is: _____

Smells, if any: _____   Drinking or eating anything: _____.

I am looking at and noticing _____ surrounding me.

Tasks I accomplished today: _____.

How accomplished I feel today: 1   2   3   4   5

I am taking a break from _____. I give myself permission to get back up and start _____ again on/at _____.

Check in to check out: What other emotions or things am I experiencing today?
_____.

My latest self-takeaway: _____.

Reflection: What do I want to remember from the last question I focused on?

_____

_____

_____

_____

_____

_____

140. What are your stressors? Make a list of current stressors. When certain stressors come up for you, how do you deal with them? Do you know when you are stressed? Did you know stress can be quiet and does not always feel like stress? How does your body tell you that it is feeling stress? What are the cues?

Set the Mood and Tone for Today's Journaling

Date and Time: _____ Location: _____.

Today my sound choice is: _____.

Smells, if any: _____ Drinking or eating anything: _____.

I am looking at and noticing _____ surrounding me.

Tasks I accomplished today: _____.

How accomplished I feel today: 1   2   3   4   5

I am taking a break from _____. I give myself permission to get back up and start _____ again on/at _____.

Check in to check out: What other emotions or things am I experiencing today?
_____.

My latest self-takeaway: _____.

Reflection: What do I want to remember from the last question I focused on?

_____
_____
_____
_____
_____
_____
_____

Recall and Recap

141. What's your edge? This edge is typically between something that causes you pain and something that is too comfortable. Where can you push yourself as you move toward a better you?

Set the Mood and Tone for Today's Journaling

Date and Time: _____ Location: _____.

Today my sound choice is: _____

Smells, if any: _____ Drinking or eating anything: _____.

I am looking at and noticing _____ surrounding me.

Tasks I accomplished today: _____.

How accomplished I feel today: 1   2   3   4   5

I am taking a break from _____. I give myself permission to get

back up and start _____ again on/at _____.

Check in to check out: What other emotions or things am I experiencing today?
_____.

My latest self-takeaway: _____.

Reflection: What do I want to remember from the last question I focused on?

_____

_____

_____

_____

_____

_____

_____

Recall and Recap

142. How are you cared for by other people? How do you want to be cared for? How do you allow yourself to be cared for? How well do you receive care when it is offered to you?

Set the Mood and Tone for Today's Journaling

Date and Time: _____ Location: _____.

Today my sound choice is: _____

Smells, if any: _____ Drinking or eating anything: _____.

I am looking at and noticing _____ surrounding me.

Tasks I accomplished today: _____.

How accomplished I feel today: 1   2   3   4   5

I am taking a break from _____. I give myself permission to get

back up and start _____ again on/at _____.

Check in to check out: What other emotions or things am I experiencing today?
_____.

My latest self-takeaway: _____.

Reflection: What do I want to remember from the last question I focused on?

_____

_____

_____

_____

_____

_____

Recall and Recap

143. What do you want to *start* doing? And, what do you want to stop doing? Make separate entries as desired. What's standing in the way of you starting or stopping these things?

Set the Mood and Tone for Today's Journaling

Date and Time: _____ Location: _____.

Today my sound choice is: _____

Smells, if any: _____ Drinking or eating anything: _____.

I am looking at and noticing _____ surrounding me.

Tasks I accomplished today: _____.

How accomplished I feel today: 1   2   3   4   5

I am taking a break from _____. I give myself permission to get

back up and start _____ again on/at _____.

Check in to check out: What other emotions or things am I experiencing today?
_____.

My latest self-takeaway: _____.

Reflection: What do I want to remember from the last question I focused on?

_____

_____

_____

_____

_____

_____

_____

Recall and Recap

144. Can you think about your life and how you may feel if you were to achieve wholeness, achieve satisfaction, and become your complete self? Write down your thoughts.

145. What stands in your way of wholeness, satisfaction, and becoming your complete self?
Write down any perceived and actual failures, setbacks, and barriers. Release the thoughts from your mind and write them down here. Now, what can you do to tackle them?

Recall and Recap

Set the Mood and Tone for Today's Journaling

Date and Time: _____ Location: _____.

Today my sound choice is: _____

Smells, if any: _____ Drinking or eating anything: _____.

I am looking at and noticing _____ surrounding me.

Tasks I accomplished today: _____.

How accomplished I feel today: 1   2   3   4   5

I am taking a break from _____. I give myself permission to get

back up and start _____ again on/at _____.

Check in to check out: What other emotions or things am I experiencing today?
_____.

My latest self-takeaway: _____.

Reflection: What do I want to remember from the last question I focused on?

_____

_____

_____

_____

_____

_____

146. What have you learned about yourself during your healing journey? How do you feel about these self-discoveries? Elaborate here. Write until you have a gentle inner pull to stop.

Set the Mood and Tone for Today's Journaling

Date and Time: _____   Location: _____.

Today my sound choice is: _____

Smells, if any: _____   Drinking or eating anything: _____.

I am looking at and noticing _____ surrounding me.

Tasks I accomplished today: _____.

How accomplished I feel today: 1   2   3   4   5

I am taking a break from _____. I give myself permission to get back up and start _____ again on/at _____.

Check in to check out: What other emotions or things am I experiencing today?
_____

My latest self-takeaway: _____.

Reflection: What do I want to remember from the last question I focused on?

_____

_____

_____

_____

_____

_____

Recall and Recap

Recall and Recap

147. What are three things you have discarded at this point in your journey? Why have you discarded—or will you discard—these three things? How do you feel now that you have done so?

Set the Mood and Tone for Today's Journaling

Date and Time: _____   Location: _____.

Today my sound choice is: _____

Smells, if any: _____ Drinking or eating anything: _____.

I am looking at and noticing _____ surrounding me.

Tasks I accomplished today: _____.

How accomplished I feel today: 1   2   3   4   5

I am taking a break from _____. I give myself permission to get

back up and start _____ again on/at _____.

Check in to check out: What other emotions or things am I experiencing today?
_____.

My latest self-takeaway: _____.

Reflection: What do I want to remember from the last question I focused on?

_____

_____

_____

_____

_____

_____

_____

Recall and Recap

148. What three thoughts are still lingering with you at this point in your journey? Why do you think these thoughts are lingering? How do these lingering thoughts make you feel? What will you do to help yourself accept or discard these thoughts down the road?

Set the Mood and Tone for Today's Journaling

Date and Time: _____　　Location: _____.

Today my sound choice is: _____.

Smells, if any: _____ Drinking or eating anything: _____.

I am looking at and noticing _____ surrounding me.

Tasks I accomplished today: _____.

How accomplished I feel today:　　1　　2　　3　　4　　5

I am taking a break from _____. I give myself permission to get

back up and start _____ again on/at _____.

Check in to check out: What other emotions or things am I experiencing today?
_____.

My latest self-takeaway: _____.

Reflection: What do I want to remember from the last question I focused on?

_____

_____

_____

_____

_____

_____

_____

_____

Recall and Recap

149. What three themes have you discovered about your life during this process? Why are these three themes important to you? Are any of these themes recurring? How does that make you feel? Are these themes you want to keep, continue exploring, or eventually discard?

Set the Mood and Tone for Today's Journaling

Date and Time: _____   Location: _____.

Today my sound choice is: _____

Smells, if any: _____   Drinking or eating anything: _____.

I am looking at and noticing _____ surrounding me.

Tasks I accomplished today: _____.

How accomplished I feel today: 1   2   3   4   5

I am taking a break from _____. I give myself permission to get back up and start _____ again on/at _____.

Check in to check out: What other emotions or things am I experiencing today?
_____.

My latest self-takeaway: _____.

Reflection: What do I want to remember from the last question I focused on?

_____

_____

_____

_____

_____

_____

Recall and Recap

150. Read this statement: "I welcome continuous healing." Does this resonate with you? If so, how? How do you plan to welcome continuous healing into your life? Write out the words that come to mind as you process your healing journey. Draw anything that comes to mind when you reflect on your continuous healing plan.

Recall and Recap

Pause Moment #8

The End of the Journal.

Take a deep breath in and slowly exhale, allowing your breath to flow effortlessly. With each inhale and exhale, take your time and deepen your breathing. Just let it flow naturally.

On the pages ahead, you will come across the ultimate Crowning Glory section, with four more questions to assess and elaborate on your journaling expedition. Take a moment to contemplate how the pieces you have put together have contributed to your overall well-being.

As you come to the end of this journaling process, it's important to remember that this is just one piece of the puzzle that makes up your entire life experience. It's not your fault that you have experienced hurt and trauma, but it's up to you to take responsibility for your healing experiences. The people who have hurt you are responsible for their actions, and you are not to blame.

It's essential to realize that you are not defined by the traumatic experience that happened to you. Your responsibility now is to focus on your healing journey and take the necessary steps to feel better and heal. While it may seem unfair, this is the truth. Remember that you have a village of people around you who care and want to support you.

CROWNING GLORY:

The best is yet to come

What advice would you give to yourself about others at this point in your journey as you reflect on what you've learned so far?

_____
_____
_____
_____
_____
_____
_____
_____

How have these prompts been helpful? What questions or topics not in this journal did you wish had been included? What questions would you add to your journey toward healing?

_____
_____
_____
_____
_____
_____
_____
_____
_____

What final piece of advice will you give yourself at this time?
And, what final piece of advice will you share with others?

_____
_____
_____
_____
_____
_____
_____

What are your final thoughts as you finish this journal?

_____
_____
_____
_____
_____
_____
_____
_____

Crowning Glory

Pause Moment #9

Self-work increases self-worth!

**Take the time to work on yourself and keep your worth at all costs. You are so worth it. If you don't think you are worth it,
who else will?**

Investing in yourself through self-work is a powerful way to boost your self-worth. It's important to take the time to work on yourself and nurture your value. Remember, you are worth it and no one else can determine your worth for you. Believe in yourself and invest in your growth.

YOUR JOURNEY CONTINUES

Thank you for joining me on this heartfelt journey of healing and for allowing me to accompany you along the way. I pray that you have received everything you needed and more. However, if there are unmet needs, remember that this journal is a tool that can be restarted as often as you like. I have included some blank pages at the end for your personal reflections.

When people come to this journal for healing, they often leave with peace, or at least more peace than when they began their journey. If this process has disrupted your peace, it is because memories are not always pleasant and can evoke challenging emotions. This is particularly true during the exercises found in the "Gather to Grow" section of questions. These tools are designed to unearth unwanted or difficult feelings. Why? So that you can learn how to grow and navigate pain that may persist as memories, gradually observing that the pain lessens over time.

Speaking of which, have you ever come across the phrase "Time heals all wounds"? Throughout my life, I have heard this phrase said countless times without fully grasping its meaning. Now, it resonates with me. As time passes, the intensity of pain diminishes into more manageable moments, allowing space for traumatic thoughts and memories to gradually lose their grip. Time, coupled with intentional healing work, can help break down the pain into digestible moments, one step at a time.

It has been my sincere pleasure to share this mindspace with you. I am genuinely delighted for your progress, and I hope that these questions and my presence in this journal have provided you with a comforting partnership as you navigate this occasionally daunting journey. Remember, I am here to support you as you venture into the shadows of healing, especially when it feels unsafe to do so alone.

I see you. I am rooting for you.

Take care,

Sheila

P.S. Remember to sign and date the following page to confirm ongoing healing.

Healing Continues with Me: _____ Date: _____

What's next for me? _____

What's the soundtrack to my life right now? Have any new songs made the cut? Have I discarded any songs that don't feel good anymore?

Here is the additional space to record the songs that helped you get through.

Go back through your journal and record the songs, silence, and other sounds that made the cut, and record them below. Use these songs to create a playlist, name it *Unapologetically Healing*, and give it a date.

Song	Artist

Song	Artist

What songs were on repeat? If it applies, write about the repeated need to hear a particular song through this process. Did you use moments of silence to get through as well? If so, what were the benefits of incorporating silence? If not, take a few moments now, in silence, to reflect on this monumental moment of healing. Whoosah!

The list of songs and artists or intentional silence or any other sounds that made the cut is the soundtrack or playlist—use the tone- and mood-setting pages to capture the full list here.

Your Journey Continues

Song	Artist

Song	Artist

Your Journey Continues

Your Journey Continues

Your Journey Continues

Your Journey Continues

Your Journey Continues

Your Journey Continues

Your Journey Continues

Your Journey Continues

Your Journey Continues

Your Journey Continues

Your Journey Continues

Your Journey Continues

Your Journey Continues

Your Journey Continues

Your Journey Continues

AUTHOR RESOURCES

As I wrap up this *Unapologetically Healing* journal, I can't help but feel grateful for the journey that brought me to this point. At times, I felt lost in a sea of pain and uncertainty, but I eventually found my way to peace and healing with the help of God, self-reflection, and the support of my loved ones. Writing this journal has been an incredibly powerful tool on my healing journey. As a young person, I longed for the perfect journal but never found one. I wrote this journal to create the kind of resource I wished I had during my adolescence and throughout my life's journey.

Working through this journal allowed me to express my emotions, track my progress, and recognize patterns, thoughts, and behaviors that have shaped my life and career. Every time I had to make corrections to bring all the elements of this journal together, I was reminded of my faith, endurance, strength, and resilience—personally and professionally. I'm grateful for the lessons I've learned, the healing I've experienced, and the growth I've achieved. Although life will always bring challenges, I'm confident that I can face them with grace, strength, and prayer.

This journal is written from my heart to yours. To anyone reading this, take the time to reflect on your journey. Whether through journaling, therapy, art, prayer, movement, laughter, tears, or any other form of expression, take time for yourself.

As I reflect on the resources that have helped me through my writing journey this past year, I would like to share a few with you. I've enjoyed Tricia Hersey's *The Nap Ministry's Rest Deck: 50 Practices to Resist Grind Culture*. I'm excited to share that I'm writing a second book called *You Are Not Your Trauma*. Although this book references female-identified gender, it speaks to anyone who has endured traumatic experiences of any kind. Remember, trauma does not discriminate.

Music has also played a significant role in my journey this year. I've listened to music from 397 artists, but 15 artists stood out and helped me through tough times. From soul and R&B to hip-hop and neo-soul, these artists kept me going when I needed it most. I spent 7,500 minutes on a particular music app, and I'm proud to say that R&B and hip-hop are my favorite genres. Suppose you're looking for some new music to add to your playlist. In that case, I highly recommend "Let It Go" by Summer Walker, "Over" by Lucky Daye, "Your Turn" by Ty Dolla $ign featuring Musiq Soulchild, "Forever Don't Last" by Jazmine Sullivan, and "So Be It" by Alex Vaughn. These are just a few of the top songs that I listened to.

Lastly, I celebrated a milestone birthday last year and enjoyed the company of fifty friends and family members on a sea voyage filled with music, fun, fellowship, and dancing. The memories that were made are priceless. One fun fact is that I compiled a complete product from a stack of Post-it notes I had collected for years. I've learned to appreciate the power of sorting, sifting, and gathering ideas to create something beautiful. I hope my journey inspires you to take action in your life, no matter your obstacles. Remember, there is strength in vulnerability, and healing is always possible.

In closing, here's a quick and final summary of what I've been up to lately . . .

As I said previously, I am writing a book titled *You Are Not Your Trauma*. This upcoming book is a comprehensive guide for anyone who has experienced trauma and wants to take steps toward healing and moving forward.

My current personal and professional daily practice includes writing, reading, noticing, and affirming. These practices and reflections help me to prioritize self-care and take time for myself. Incorporating these practices with intentionality is an excellent way for anyone who wants to integrate moments of rest into their daily routine.

Here is a list of recommended readings that have inspired and helped me on my healing journey. Each book includes a summary of why I found it beneficial.

- *Born a Crime* is Trevor Noah's autobiographical book about growing up mixed-race in apartheid South Africa. The book is a poignant reflection on his experiences navigating racial segregation, trauma, poverty, and violence.

- *Rest Is Resistance* is a movement founded by Tricia Hersey that promotes rest and self-care to resist constant societal pressure to be productive. Hersey's work creates spaces and resources that encourage people to prioritize self-care to prevent burnout and promote overall well-being.

- The King James Version of the Bible is a widely read and beloved book of the Holy Scriptures.

- *A Piece of Cake* is a memoir by Cupcake Brown that tells the story of her journey through addiction, abuse, and homelessness to recovery and redemption. The book explores Brown's difficult early life and her ultimate triumph over these challenges through faith, perseverance, and the support of others. It is a powerful and inspiring story of personal growth and resilience.

- *My Pretty and Its Ugly Truth* is a powerful memoir by De'Vonna Bentley-Pittman that explores themes of colorism, self-acceptance, and resilience. Through her personal story, she offers valuable insights into how readers can learn to love and accept themselves despite societal pressures.

- *The Band-Aid Bond* by Grace Cornish is a practical guide that helps readers break patterns of unhealthy loving and build healthy relationships. The book provides real-life examples and insights into why people may be attracted to unhealthy relationships.

- *In the Meantime* by Iyanla Vanzant is a book that offers practical advice for navigating periods of waiting and uncertainty. Through personal stories and guidance, readers can develop a deeper understanding of themselves and find peace during difficult times.

- *5 Essential Principles for Healing Black Men and Raising Black Boys* by Dr. Kasim Abdur Razzaq provides practical advice and strategies to help Black men and boys overcome trauma. The book's five essential principles are valuable tools for healing and growth.

You may find the following podcasts supportive and helpful:

- *Gettin' Grown* is a humorous and insightful podcast where hosts Jade and Keia discuss the challenges of adulthood, including mental health, personal growth, and career development.

- *All Black Men Need Therapy* is a podcast hosted by mental health professionals that explores mental health challenges Black men face. It covers topics such as depression, anxiety, and trauma and aims to promote self-care and destigmatize talking about mental health.

- *The Redefining Wealth Podcast with Patrice Washington* believes wealth is about more than money and material possessions; it's about well-being.
- *LifeTalk* with Michelle McKinney Hammond is a candid and empowering podcast hosted by a bestselling author, international speaker, spiritual leader, and relationship expert.

Great news! I'm also cultivating an affirmation card deck that will include a variety of positive affirmations and empowering messages. The main goal of this deck is to help individuals develop self-love, confidence, and inner peace. I'm excited to share it with everyone! Here's a sneak peek of some of the affirmations you can expect in this upcoming project. So, stay tuned!

These affirmations are intended to encourage you to reflect on your personal journey and consider how they may positively impact your life.

- **I affirm that despite the worries in my life, I am advancing and flourishing**. I recognize that my edge is where I find my strength. My edge is between comfort and suffering. I am capable of advantageously conquering any obstruction. I am comforted by those who have cared for me. I am committed to caring for others simultaneously. I practice benevolence.

- **I am dedicated to becoming a whole self and will continue learning**. I will pray and ask for what I need. I appropriate what is given in return. I take a quiet pause and boisterous breath, allowing myself to sit in the wonderment of "what else can I do to continue this path of cultivation and self-exploration?" I was designed to be whole. I was intended to be healed. My arrears have been paid.

- **Healing continues with me!** I am the salt of the earth. I am my assignment. I am my tasks. I am not perfect, yet I am connected to the one who is—wholeness, health, and healing are my birthrights to claim. Healing doesn't stop with me; it continues as a journey. I embody healing! I am a new pathway for generational healing experiences. I am healthy.

Where can you connect with me? Well, you can find me on my author website at **www.DrSheilaSweeney.com**. You can also catch me on LinkedIn, Instagram, and Facebook by searching for my username: **@drsheilasweeney**. And if you're into TikTok, you can follow me there too!

What other resources will support you and your journey? Use the following space to collect your own library of resources.

ACKNOWLEDGMENTS

I am grateful as I take a moment to express my thanks to the many people who supported and encouraged me throughout the writing process. Without your contributions, this book would not have been possible.

First and foremost, I want to thank God, my family, my friends, and my church for their unwavering love and support throughout my healing and writing journey. Your belief in me has inspired and motivated me to keep going, even when the going got tough. Dad and Alene, I know you would be proud of me. Even though you are not here to see the finished project, you were incredibly instrumental in getting this project to the finish line. Your words of encouragement from memories ago kicked in at just the right time, and I am forever grateful for your existence within me.

To Peaces 'n PuzSouls: Journeys thru Healing community: I am grateful for your support of my organization and any way you have been connected to it. Our work and conversations inspired this journal, as I created Post-it notes for every reflection and thought gained, ultimately creating something that I hope you can be proud of. Thank you for being my inspiration and motivation.

I am grateful to Wise Ink's Writing on Purpose group for your support, encouragement, and listening ear during the writing process. Our writer's retreat lit the fire to a blaze, and I'm so happy to have met and connected with all of you.

I thank my beta listeners—mostly friends, family, and strangers (lol)—for your invaluable feedback and insights during the pre-publication process. Your feedback, listening ears, and suggestions helped me refine and make the book the best for the community. Thank you for being my crew, village, and support system through and through!

I want to express my heartfelt gratitude to all those who supported and contributed to the creation of this book at and through my publisher, Wise Ink Media. Thank you to the proofreaders and those who had possible roles I don't know about!

- Dara, thank you for putting it all together, for your publishing expertise, for coordinating everything, and for listening to my vision from the start. We eventually got to where we wanted to arrive, and I couldn't have done it without you.

- Sara, thank you for your editorial expertise. You made everything make sense when my brain couldn't quite put it together correctly. Your passion for journals was everything, and you made that come across in your work.

- Janay, I knew you would be an excellent fit for the design, and you have made this work come alive with your visionary skills. You are super DOPE!

- The marketing professionals at Wise Ink, Hanna, and Crown, your expertise has been invaluable. Hanna, I have learned a lot from you, including marketing office hours!

- Vivian, thank you for holding it down in multiple parts of this project, especially interior design. You got me from the jump, and I appreciate that.

- Amy, during the retreat, you helped me flesh out my idea further.

- For all those doing your greatness behind the scenes—thank you too! All your work and dedication have meant a lot to me, and I am grateful.

To those who are authors or aspiring authors: it is worth it. You all have a story to share, and somebody is waiting to hear it. The process is slow and daunting, with a lot of hurry-up-and-wait moments. However, once you understand that, you can rest assured that your whole body of work will be birthed at the right time with the right team and on the correct birthdate.

Last but never least, for you, dear reader, reading this part here, at the very end: thank you for supporting this project. Your support means everything to me.

Peace, Light, and Love,

Dr. Sheila Sweeney, LICSW